Bringing Down Sales Barriers and Challenges

A Road Map for Closing More Deals Faster!

RAMIN ELAHI

*To my mom, for keeping world history alive
with her masterful storytelling*

*To my dad, the ultimate practitioner of Habit One—continuously
augmenting his circle of influence and friends*

And

To my aunt, uncles, and Behzad for all their riveting stories!

Table of Contents

Introduction

In this book, I will share some of my twenty-plus years of technical training and sales & marketing experience. From experience, I know it is challenging for those of us with technical backgrounds to walk into a sales conversation and focus effectively on the return-on-investment (ROI) and other business-related issues that matter the most to the customer. Instead, many of us- out of our comfort zone- merely focus on technical details of our solution. Making that change requires a major shift in our mindset. I hope this book addresses those challenges, especially for those new to sales. For veteran salespeople (both technical and non-technical) and sales team leaders there will also be plenty of valuable pointers and refreshers in the form of lessons learned throughout this book.

I walked into the sales world by responding to a job posting for an applications engineer. Almost immediately, the job title and the nature of the job became two different things. As a recent college graduate with an advanced degree and a few years of research building an Algebraic Systolic Processor (an *Acousto-Optic* version of it, mind you!), I was not able to land a job more in line with my background—even during the booming job market of early '90s. At the same time, the co-owners of this particular computer peripheral company were having no success hiring additional sales staff. So, the combination of an attractive job ad and my willingness to apply for any engineering job came together.

With no prior sales or marketing experience, I thought I had been hired to troubleshoot customers' problems with our newly released SCSI (Small Computer System Interface) hard disks and tape drives, or perhaps optimize their Unix operating systems to work better with the external RAM (random access memory) modules. In reality, my job was to sell these peripherals and other computer accessories; the users were buying them back then to *soup up* their computers.

Within a few days on the job, I recognized my lack of sales knowledge and started to read sales books; some were classics, and some had catchier, *get-rich-fast* titles. Although they were helpful to some extent, I needed a mentor, coach, or at least a book or an article to guide me on some of the common challenges a salesperson faces from the start of a deal to its closing. I needed to understand the challenges like which landmines not to step on during the course of a deal or even just general best practices. Yes, of course, everyone told me the most obvious stuff like: "Conduct yourself politely and professionally over the phone," or "Always apologize in advance if they hate your prices."

I appreciated the advice, but it wasn't exactly consistent. I heard conflicting advice on giving discounts or when to stand my ground on pricing, etc. What I really needed went above and beyond these overstated "to cook, you need water" type suggestions. I needed practical and effective guidance on how to best serve my customers.

In the chapters that follow, through stories about my first job, I hope to provide you with the insights I desperately needed when I started selling.

Regardless of how many years of commercial sales you have, your experiences so far surely have convinced you that a sale is not an *event* but a *process*. Based on this premise, the main objectives of this book are threefold.

First, the goal is to get you out of the comfortable box lined with the proverbial *shoulds* and *musts* of selling and into the *realities* of obvious and hidden barriers at each stage of the sales cycle. Every salesperson claims that if the buyer is desperate and is in an immediate dire need, selling a product or service is a *no-brainer*. That is, a purchase order (PO) is drafted in a jiffy for an attractive price the vendor wishes to charge, followed by the delivery as soon as the initial or full deposit is secured. However, the same people can tell you these opportunities are few and far in between. Just like anything else, there is structure and steps in conducting a sale, which is called the Sales Process or Sales Cycle. It typically includes five to eight phases depending on product and how the seller's and buyer's companies pursue opportunities. But let us first define the typical phases of the sales process which we will follow throughout the book:

1) Prospecting
2) Initial discovery and needs assessment
3) Qualification
4) Solution presentation
5) Preparing for objections
6) Negotiation
7) Deal closure

With each phase, there are numerous challenges and barriers that you and your sales team will face, which this book will expose and provide guidance on. Regardless of how many phases and under which names—which vary from one industry to another—both the seller and buyer will have to navigate through these phases—some implicitly and others explicitly—before they can close a deal.

Of course, many people view processes as a burden or something that slows progress. Others may go as far as calling it *process paralysis,* which is a phenomenon that describes the state that teams suffer when they must follow an overbearing organizational processes. Hence, in effect, paralyzing progress. Skipping parts of the process may be a valid tactic when customers are lining up for your products and services during a buoyant market. However, many sales experts strongly believe that this process can save you during any sales cycle regardless of the state of the market at the time. In other words, process before content. So, trust the process!

Second, there are volumes of books available, online or in print, which describe the theory and essentials of the sales process in more depth; hence, this book will not attempt to provide the same level of philosophical definition and repeat the geneses of each phases. Instead, this book will uniquely present the challenges and realities of each phase in an incisive format of *Problem-Solution-Payoff*. Never before has the sheer volume of sales and marketing messages bombarding prospects been greater, and the selling environment has never been noisier or more cluttered than we see today. So, how do we arm our sales teams with the most effective messaging possible? How do we ensure that our sales and marketing messages will actually cut through the clutter, distinguish our offerings, and move the sales process forward? Well, this format of *problem-solution-payoff* is the most effective method of promoting or selling a service, product, or even an idea in today's selling climate where the commercial messages have become increasingly clichéd, indistinguishable, and loaded with corporate jargon and meaningless platitudes.

As the salesperson or marketer, your chances are much better if you provide a vision for your buyer of overcoming their current *challenges* with your *solution*. And as a result, *the payoff* will be achieving, doing, gaining something greater, better, and higher. This is why, at the start of each chapter, we state the current problems (or challenges) associated with each phase and clearly identify some possible solutions which I believe will pay off.

Over the course of writing this book, extensive research led to some valuable stories, analysis, and testimonials that consummate sales and marketing professionals from the trenches of sales and customer-facing events to the C-suites shared with me. Their experience and lessons learned provide key guidance on how to overcome most of the barriers so that your sales cycles become shorter and you achieve your sales quotas faster. It is a common belief amongst all cultures that the "experiences of others are quite the gift." But only if the receiver is open and subsequently pays attention to the presenter. As Malcom Gladwell puts it: "Authors are theory poor but experience rich."

Third, this book is to reintroduce salespeople to the concept of *Situational Fluency*. I first came across this mouthful when I took part in a Solution Selling workshop many years ago facilitated by one of its developers and author, Michael Bosworth. According to him, *Situational Fluency* is the integration of knowledge and skills. Its main components are the inter-related circles of 1) Situation Knowledge, 2) Capability Knowledge, 3) People Skills, and 4) Selling Skills.

Also, as we navigate through the content of this book, you will be exposed to many best practices that are required for a successful sale. One of which is this *situational fluency that the seller needs to possess to integrate their business and technical knowledge with the communication skills to keep you aligned with your buyer.*

The Other Main Goal of This Book:

There was a study by Steve W. Martin (not the wild and crazy and the talented actor but the author and professor from the USC Marshall School of Business) which consisted of interviewing 230-plus buyers. His research reported that 12 percent of salespeople are excellent, 23 percent good, 38 percent average, and close to a third poor. When I read the study, I immediately flashed back to my first account and business development (ABD) workshop a few years earlier.

Also, apropos to the above research, another study reveals that 81 percent of buyers indicated they would rather talk with someone who shares their mannerisms. That is, buyers will choose sales-people who develop *rapport* over those who don't. So, when I went back to my ABD workshop notes, I came across the simple drawing depicted in Figure I below, which explains graphically the core message of the above survey perfectly!

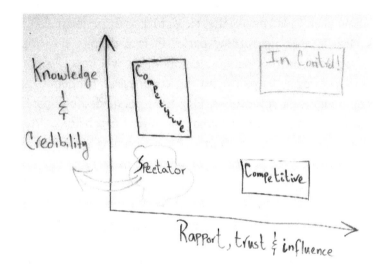

Figure I.

While we will cover a slew of sales challenges, this book will also emphasize behaviors that can help any salesperson *control* the sales process by building the rapport, trust, and influence needed with potential customers. Without taking the time to build these essential elements, the best one can become—before ending up on the sideline as a spectator—is merely *competitive*, winning or losing depending on the relative strengths and weaknesses of your competition.

Also, going forward, as the COVID pandemic and lockdown continues to loom over every aspect of our lives and businesses, more and more business transactions will take place in a hybrid manner (i.e., parts in face-to-face and parts virtually) or all done virtually. The annual CEO Benchmarking Report 2021 released by Predictive Index—an organization that offers workforce assessments solutions—said 97 percent of CEOs will allow some degree of remote work moving forward. "Teams aren't just new—they're virtual; and for most CEOs, it's clear there's no turning back." In fact, despite the hope and expectation that economic conditions will improve once the world begins to exit from the coronavirus pandemic, the many benefits of remote working have persuaded companies to invest further in their virtual and digital capabilities. While the experts and sales organizations are coming up with playbooks on the best practices for effective delivery of some of each phase's tasks being done remotely, throughout this book, many of the challenges are identified and the new trends to stay competitive virtually will be introduced. That is because the only silver lining in these gloomy pandemic days is that the coronavirus has already spurred investment and encouraged innovation and efficiency in many of the sales cycle's phases.

At the Risk of Ruining the Ending...

Let us see what is at stake at the first phase of the sales process.

Prospecting (or Sales Inquiry) is the core, the foundation, the heart of every sales cycle and consists of finding a legitimate potential customer. Simply stated, if there is no customer, there shall be no sale. At the same time, selling has become increasing difficult. All in all, the main challenge of this phase is "can we win their business?" If so, at what cost? For example, does your solution or offering fully fits their needs? Who's driving their effort and why is it important to them to consider your product and service? In this stage, you present yourself as a trusted advisor. Once you've built a solid relationship with the person driving the change your solution is well equipped to facilitate, you will have an inside coach who can teach you more about how to gain a competitive advantage and provide insights into the existing relationships between your prospect and their incumbent suppliers.

Sales and marketing are two different entities that must always compliment and supplement each other. Often, when these two teams are not in synch about who the prospect is and how and when to close a deal, it creates enormous challenges and frustration for both teams. To align sales and marketing missions and visions with each other, customers, and potential customers, experts like the trusted advisors at the Future Today Institute emphasize the following strategic planning framework. That is, instead of each team arbitrarily and independently assigning goals on quarterly or annual timelines, they recommend using the cone format shown in Figure 2 to plan a more coordinated approach.

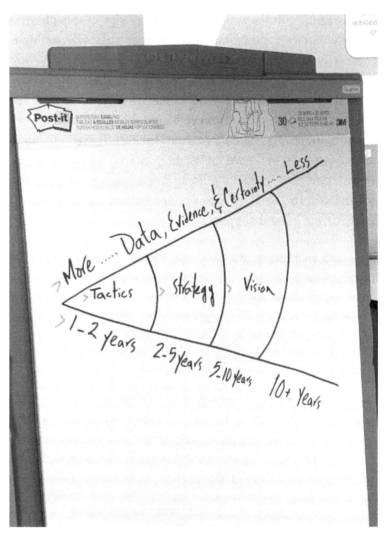

Figure 2.

Of course, the timeline varies for every project and sales opportunity; however, the cone framework is an improvement over the typical time and Gantt charts, as experts believe we must continually recalibrate our organization's vision for the future.

In the Initial Meeting Phase, you help prospects explore and recognize their current and future needs and challenges. During this phase and others, the challenge for the seller is to remove uncertainty and concerns about potential risks from buyer's mind. However, the first challenge in this phase is ensuring they like you. According to a *Harvard Business Review* article, "Before people decide what they think of your message they decide what they think of you."

Be ready to present yourself as a trusted advisor and be able to expand your situational fluency to gain the respect and trust of your prospects. What matters most to potential customers are the pains and gains, penalties and rewards, losses and profits, negative or positive implications of going or not going with your product or service. Also, in this chapter we will identify the "outside-in" strategy as the best approach to make the customer aware of their current challenges and pains.

Need analysis identifies gaps between current and ideal or desired circumstances. Note that there is a direct correlation between successful deals and the numbers of interactions you have with senior leadership. Winners are those who are able to talk about their products and/or services on multiple levels— i.e., from just describing the product's primary features and benefits to going deep under the hood to fully describe your solution depending on the potential customer's needs.

In the Qualification round, the challenge is to ask qualification questions that will provide needed information as to whether the deal is worth pursuing further. This phase serves as a steppingstone toward a successful closing in a timely manner without compromising your or your customer's needs. In Chapter Three, the key challenges are not responding to the answers prospects provide to your BANT (Budget, Authority, Need, and Time) questions; instead, focus on open questions you will use to clarify their situation with respect to the BANT items.

Chapter Four is about **presenting** your solution to your potential buyer and perhaps their management and other stakeholders. Remember to show empathy for your audience who are not as well versed on the technical details of your presentation. Be aware that they may be more interested in the ROI and other payoffs of your solution. Thus, your presentation must be complemented and supplemented by the support of your internal *champion* who's fighting on your behalf from within the potential customer's organization.

In the *initial meeting phase*, we outlined the difficulty of securing an initial appointment with executives and decision-makers. Once there, either virtually or in-person, you must know and be able to clearly express your solution, with your core message addressing their current pain. The top producers are *communication chameleons* who master both the neuro-linguistic and psychological frameworks essential to better connect with customers. For example, numbers are a great way to show potential buyers the benefits of your offerings; however, your presentation needs to include relatable details to stand up to the buyers' scrutiny.

Also, in this chapter you will be reminded that the salesforce of tomorrow must embrace the realities of virtual presentations.

According to Bain & Company, a global management consultancy firm, virtual B2B (business to business) selling is here to stay—even beyond the era of COVID. Their research shows that virtual presentations have "greater effectiveness," "improved customer experience," and "reduced costs." Therefore, there is a dedicated section in this chapter on the challenges and best practices of virtual presentations. Once you have presented your solutions successfully and decision-makers have internalized what you told them, chances are high you will be called back for the next phase, which is when you will address their more specific, information-based potential *objections* or *concerns*.

In Chapter Five, we will make you aware of the most common **objections** raised by customers. You will see that budget is the most common reason stronger sales opportunities fall apart. Price is the first thing most buyers look at. Your chief challenge in this phase is to avoid taking customer objections personally. Although it is easier said than done, objections should motivate you, not discourage or offend. Winston Churchill said, "Kites rise highest against the wind." That is to say, overcoming resistance is needed when you are going for great.

Also, we'll see that ignoring or dismissing buyers' concerns and/or objections could seriously derail talks. In other words, when you don't hear and understand the customer's concerns, you may be missing the key points and completely misunderstand their concerns. Listen carefully, actively and repeat back to them their concerns regarding price, quality, delivery time, terms, etc.

In **Chapter Six**, we will look at the **Negotiation Phase** because when objections are not resolved, the negotiation phase begins. Remember, your customers face increased competition in their own markets and must focus on pricing, quality, and delivery pressures daily. Despite improved customer relationships, the pricing pressures they face and buyers' access to information about other offerings will always lead to numerous challenges. For example, to avoid delays, the salesperson must recognize the customer's negotiation methods and react correctly by using a professional approach, like leading the customer back to the mutually beneficial alternatives you have to offer.

In closing, we reach the **Deal Closure Phase**. **Chapter Seven** describes the logical conclusion of all the earlier phases—whether it be reaching a deal or being derailed from it. If the latter, you owe it to yourself and your sales and marketing teams to do a postmortem review to see what went wrong and document the lessons learned, so that future deals may be more successful. And if the former, perhaps soccer enthusiasts relate to this quote by Sepp Herberger, the legendary head coach of West Germany's national team in the '50s, on how to up your game for the next opportunity: "After the game is before the game."

Finally, when businesses provide aftermarket support, they gain a deep understanding of customers' technologies, processes, and plans—knowledge rivals can't easily acquire—that provides a sustainable, competitive advantage and can lead to a continuous source of income and profit.

As I said earlier, even with little sales experience or coming from a technical background, you should have encountered many of these concepts and challenges in the past. The object is to recognize your own experience, find learning resources, build your knowledge, and learn the phases of a successful sales process. You will get better by practicing the skills needed for each phase and the strategies described in this book, and this repetition will help you in consistently *Bringing Down Sales Barriers and Challenges*.

As a teacher, trainer, and coach, I see the path to perfection is paved with *repetition*. That is, in every great culture and language of the world we can find this adage that says, "Amateurs practice until they get it right; professionals practice until they can't get it wrong."

So, I hope this book provides a valuable foundation and roadmap for how to build perfection. By repeatedly using and refining the skills and knowledge herein, and deploying these skills within each selling opportunity, you will succeed.

Happy Selling!

CHAPTER 1

Prospecting Phase

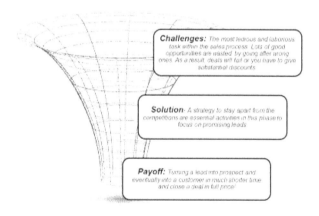

Challenges: The most tedious and laborious task within the sales process. Lots of good opportunities are wasted by going after wrong ones. As a result, deals will fall or you have to give substantial discounts

Solution: A strategy to stay apart from the competitions are essential activities in this phase to focus on promising leads

Payoff: Turning a lead into prospect and eventually into a customer in much shorter time and close a deal in full price!

Customers From Heaven

The tale of customer and business relationships is as old as buying and selling. No business—regardless of its size—can exist without customers. As I alluded to in the introduction, my very first sales experience was like a fairy tale. On my first day, as soon as my boss Janet showed me my desk, the phone rang. Janet told me to take it. While I stumbled to greet the caller and properly introducing myself, Janet pointed to the customer greeting cheat sheet by my right hand—laminated, no less—and opened the products and services catalogue near my left hand—the one she had briefly gone over with me moments earlier during my hour-long orientation.

It turned out I had the customer at *Hello*. Yes, without even properly identifying myself and explaining what we sold, the guy on the other end of the line asked me about our price and the availability of a certain 100MB Wren 5.25-inch disk drive made by Control Data Corporation (CDC—this was before Seagate bought CDC) that he had seen in a trade magazine. While I read from our sales cheat sheet, the caller turned into a customer and placed an order for two of those drives—$1,200!

In the moment, I did not realize what had happened. Later on, when I was briefed by management about the sales margins, base, and threshold prices, I found out that the firm had scored a 135 percent margin on my first sale. The profit margins were very high for such commodity gadgets in those days. At that point, I thought the phones would ring with eager customers on the other end of the line every day, and *bingo*—customers would place hefty orders for computer peripherals and all we had to do was collect payment and ship them out. Under this delusion, I did not understand the fuss about cold calling and prospecting. Or why the boss and other salespeople congratulated me after my very first call.

From then on, every day, as I made my daily cold sales calls to the people in the Rolodex or on the weekly lead sheet, it became evident that a sale on my first day was a beginner's luck. For the next thirty days, I could not sell a thing. Nothing. Nada. Zip.

Essentials of Prospecting

Selling is not an event; it is a process. I did not know this back in the '90s—let alone what prospecting or sale cycles were all about. Thinking about it now, I'm not even sure the owners of that mom-and-pop shop had any clue about them either. Every week, a guy would come to the office and hand a few pages of leads to the owners. The names on the lists were divided and eventually ended up on the inside salespeople's desks. From there, using the leased WATTS (Wide-Area Telephone Service Provider) lines, I and the other two sellers would call the leads indiscriminately—whether they were hot or cold.

Connecting the dots now, it makes sense that bringing in new clients is essential to the health of every business. Which also makes prospecting the most difficult and time-consuming phase of the sale process. If you don't do it right, you can't get to the next phases. It is an understatement to say prospecting is the most difficult and time-consuming activity for any sales professional.

Remember, as a salesperson your *ultimate* goal is to close a deal, but more importantly, the *immediate* goal is to get to the next phase of the sales process. Thus, to sell a product or service, you must first have a prospective buyer. Although there is no dream prospect or customer, salespeople need some idea of who's interested in their products. Many books discuss classical and contemporary aspects of prospecting. For example, Paul Cherry in his book *Question that Sell* alludes to the fact that developing any relationship is a process, something that takes time and effort. Both at the personal and corporate level, trying to force or manipulate a relationship into a specific timeframe can backfire and cause one or both of the parties involved to leave the relationship.[1]

In sales, each company, industry, or product has its own processes and cycles lasting from a few weeks to years. Buyers also have their own buying cycles of biding and procurement that salespeople should be mindful of. All sales and marketing relationships require some level of trust. To cultivate trust and success, as a salesperson you need to invest time in the process by asking the right questions of your prospective clients. Active listening is just as important as asking challenging questions. Per Pope Benedict XVI, "Listening is one of the toughest jobs." This is particularly true when you as a salesperson know that you have the right solution and can't wait to show the potential customer how it works.

By questioning and listening carefully to the answers, salespeople can thoroughly demonstrate their *ethos* and *logos*. Aristotle coined both terms and they mean to convince prospects of your credibility and logic, respectively. Doing so will instill confidence and trust in prospective clients, which is the foundation upon which to build powerful business relationships.

Inbound and Outbound Prospecting Leads

To set the stage for the sales cycle, it is necessary to define some key sales roles. Sales Development Representative (SDR) or Business Development Representative (BDR) are typically early sales roles that focus on generating leads. An SDR focuses on prospecting outbound leads while a BDR focuses on qualifying inbound leads generated by marketing. Regardless of roles, educating our sales teams effectively is a major challenge. Much of the current classical and contemporary books on sales are often conspicuously silent on the day-to-day challenges and landmines salespeople face.

What Are the Challenges?

In this era of digital marketing and online shopping, there are numerous challenges in finding ideal prospects and making them into potential customers. Because, "Selling has become increasingly more difficult. Prospects have less time and yet decision makers are on the receiving end of more sales calls than ever before. With a boom in the number of products being offered, 'No' is the most prevalent response right off the bat."[2] Thus, it can't be overstated—prospecting is *the* most difficult part of the sales process.

Equally so, this chapter took the longest to write and review because it had to be right, because prospecting done right will eventually lead to closing deals faster and without discounts. Although many of these terms are used interchangeably, the progression of a typical target client is this: 1) Lead, 2) Suspect, 3) Prospect, 4) Customer.

The challenges are enormous. Many salespeople use the *Productive Selling* method, getting into their sales pitch by telling the prospect the following information in sequence: 1) Company name, 2) Product, Features, and 3) Pricing, etc. In other words, the sellers follow the unwritten rule of ABC (always be closing). This is the most convenient approach for the seller. However, this effortless approach will only work if you have no competition and you talk to the prospect at the right time and place, when they have immediate need of a product or solution like yours.

Instead of following the transactional ABC approach, put your consultative selling hat on by aiming for ABH (always be helping) and digging into prospects' needs, expectations, possible benefits of using your solution—the payoff and RIO for them if they go with you. The goal of this approach is to start a conversation with the prospect so you can get to the next phase.

Here are few challenges associated with the prospecting phase:

1. Too Many Leads/Opportunity Prioritization (Sales Qualified Leads)

Today, with the proliferation of channels and sources, too many sales leads are being generated. The people compiling these leads swear by their information and claim they are all "keepers." However, these *keepers* are not always as promised. Having tons of leads in the pipeline is analogous to having a big, fat sewer pipe.

Instead, ideally, we should always aim for a fountain with clear water. To find a suitable prospect for our product or service, we need to have the necessary alignment between the sales and marketing teams. Their successful collaboration will lead to more promising sales qualified leads (SQL).

We will talk more about the qualification phase later. For now, here's what Shaun Karamdashti, Sales

Engineering (SE) Sr. Manager at Oracle, said about the leads:

> We have this intuitive classification of leads into three tiers of cold, warm, and hot leads. Traditionally, the function of pipeline generation and lead development have often been given to a different group (sales development reps, SDR, or business development, BDR). It is important to build metrics and compensation plans for these groups to align with the front-end salespeople. One real-life example is at a cloud-based software company, SDRs and BDRs were compensated based on targets downloading or using products on a free trial basis. This often resulted in thousands of leads where prospects were convinced to download and free trial (just to get rid of a pushy SDR). As soon as the compensation of these groups was changed to getting paid on actual sales orders the hit rate improved. It even got better when the compensation was aligned to the prospect consuming services even after signing the order. This way of thinking can easily separate the leads into cold, warm, and hot leads and allows better prioritization of sales teams' efforts.

2. Dealing with Resistance and Early Objections

Later, we will discuss the most common resistance and objections seen during each phase of the sales process in detail. For now, please understand, you really can't blame prospects for identifying your motive quickly. You can't afford to be unprepared to deal with these proverbial excuses—after all, all they want to do is get off the phone:

- I'm sorry but busy right now.
- Is this a sales call?
- I'm not interested.
- Just send me some info.
- We already have someone for that.
- We are not looking to make any changes right now.
- We don't have a budget/money to spend.
- Call me back in X months.

Of course, each of these reasons could be valid.

With so much information out there, prospects know they can search for a solution when they are ready to buy. However, if you present yourself as someone who can guide them in navigating the abundance of information and subsequently help them make the right decision, you will earn *trusted advisor status* with them. Remember, the game plan at this phase is finding an opportunity for another meeting in which you can tell them more about your offerings.

3. Creating a Targeted Prospecting Strategy

Prior to developing a targeted prospecting strategy, it is essential that the marketing team outlines its strategic goals, as illustrated in Figure 3, the model was first proposed by Pat Rocco of Advantage Media. In essence, to succeed in this endeavor, it is essential to have effective and targeted sales and marketing strategies, where the former is the exchange of value and the latter is getting someone interested in making that exchange.

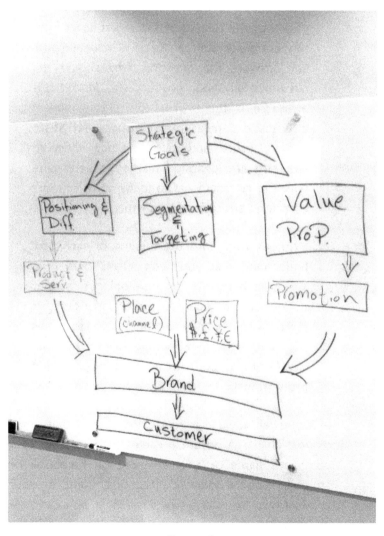

Figure 3.

To briefly review the contents of the boxes in Figure 3: *Positioning* is determining the distinctive place you want your product to occupy; *Differentiation* is designing your product offering so it has one or more unique qualities valued by the customer that sets it apart from the competition's products; a *value proposition* answers the question, why should the customer buy your product; and *Market segmentation* is the process of splitting buyers into distinct, measurable groups that share similar wants and needs. Once different segments are identified, marketers determine which target segments to focus on to support corporate strategy and growth.

Without going into the minutia of each box, understand that your company should have a similar blueprint for developing strategies to attract and retain customers. Marketing is tasked with defining expectations and activities within each box and should follow the classic *4Ps* of marketing (product, place, price, and promotions).

In a nutshell, *inbound sales* are those sales that come to you. That is, a potential client/customer saw your company's name or advertisement on Facebook or stumbled upon a valuable piece of content, or your product was mentioned in a credible publication— which led them to contact you. These are nice, warm leads that turn into clients rather quickly. Whereas *outbound sales* are sales you go out and find. In this model, the salesperson reaches out and speaks with leads. In general, outbound sales allows companies to introduce their product or service to potential customers who might not have found the company on their own.

When comparing the two, inbound sales are newer and shinier than their counterparts; nevertheless, both need to work together to achieve maximum sales through various sales and marketing campaigns.

Today's marketplace, marketing strategy, and sales strategy are on the move. Marketing focuses on generating inbound calls rather than cold calling leads. Today, most forward-thinking sales organizations focus on inside sales strategies. These strategies are well developed and implemented when they are data-driven, with highly engaged sales reps, and strategies that continuously evolve as the business changes.

Over the last decade, sales methods have changed drastically from face-to-face (F2F), in-office visits to generating lists of phone numbers and casting a wide net online to find prospects. However, for many vendors and suppliers, their strategies have not kept up with the changes.

Without any hyperbole or speculation, today, if we ask ten salespeople or sales managers about strategy, we would likely get at least ten different methods or best practices, all based upon the individual's good and bad experiences, resources, and comfort zone. Some would find an *outbound sales* strategy more effective while others may prefer *inbound sales* due to their limited resources.

4. Enabling the Sales Enablement Team

One primary force behind any sales organization is their Sales Enablement Team. The sales enablement work to enhance seller visibility within their target audience and identifies the issues these prospects face. By doing research, the enablement team develops an executable strategy based on both inbound and outbound sales methodologies. The resources and assets the sales enablement team produces must be: 1) foundational, 2) continuous, 3) transformational, and 4) reactive. The whole idea is to get the right people into the right conversations with the right decision-makers in the right ways. This will enhance the capability of the sales team to pursue more practical ideas through scalable and repeatable practices. These basic sales support strategies can be implemented or reinforced by:

- Building long-term roles, specific tools, processes, and best practices which are scalable and repeatable. This can be done by partnering with the sales team to agree upon specific goals, deliverables, milestones, and responsibilities.
- Driving better conversations and achieving higher conversion rates by facilitating seller and buyer access to on-demand, in-context, high-quality product information.

- Gaining full understanding of customer behavior by using cloud-based technology that tracks views of branded content.
- Eliminating silos and bubbles that tend to convey conflicting messages to prospective buyers.
- Prospecting activity from the top of the funnel and continuously pouring new leads into the funnel.

Also, one of the lessons learned in this COVID-19 era is to increase the digital skill sets in sales organizations. Particularly, there is a need for more virtual sales enablement. According to a Gartner Group report titled "The Future of Sales," "this includes actions for sales enablement in areas such as sales skills, training delivery and onboarding to support sellers in a virtual sales environment and equip them to effectively sell in a remote setting." Thus, the sales organizations will need to adjust their existing investments and reallocate resources among people, processes, and technology to support digital, hybrid, and virtual selling.

5. Getting Appointments and Capturing the Prospect's Attention is Difficult

With too many leads, it is impossible to find time and resources to follow up and engage with every prospect. With such an overload, either you would give up or the right prospects will stop communicating with you. No one likes poor or delayed follow-up; thus, if you have a backlog of calls, it is likely prospects will either stay with incumbent suppliers or go to your competition.

On the other side of the coin, getting prospects to agree to a meeting has become more and more challenging. A Corporate Executive Board (CEB) study of more than 1,400 business to business customers found, nearly 60 percent of typical purchasing decisions—which include researching solutions, ranking options, setting requirements, benchmarking pricing, and so on—are made before having a conversation with a supplier:

> In this world, the celebrated "solution sales rep" can be more of an annoyance than an asset. Customers in an array of industries, from IT to insurance to business process outsourcing, are often way ahead of the salespeople who are helping them.[3]

More focused research, a better understanding of industry challenges, and relevant messaging will lead to more successful prospecting. No matter how you're communicating with prospects, your message needs to be compelling. Remember, only 2 or 3 percent of your prospects will respond to email. Thus, to move your prospects to respond, you first need to develop a messaging strategy. One single email or phone call won't be enough to grab their attention. Rather, send out a series of communications that speak to a certain challenge or trends your prospects face, which can be used in both inbound and outbound sales.

Keep prospects engaged in the early stages of contact by providing valuable and relevant information by understanding their industry and needs. Don't start by telling them how awesome your company is or playing on tentative relationships—for example, we both belong to the same club, gym, or honor society.

Delivering the right message to the right person at the right time will dramatically increase response rates. Research by Target Marketing Systems in Atlanta, Georgia, shows that cold calling is the least successful method of gaining access to prospects. For example, in one survey, 80 percent of respondents said they would never or only occasionally talk to salespeople making cold calls. Moreover, an email sent out before the call is not likely to improve the odds of a meeting either. By far, the most effective means of getting on an executive's calendar is an inside recommendation.

In the same survey, 84 percent of respondents indicated they would usually or always grant meetings with a salesperson based on a recommendation from inside their firm.[4]

One of the most effective ways to squeeze into your prospect's organization and gain influence is by finding a *champion*. "Although champions are not the ultimate decision makers, and they rarely have substantial power within their organization, they have four things that make them irreplaceable in developing and closing the deal: credibility, connections, company intelligence, and motivation," according to Paul Weinstein, a Silicon Valley-based investment banker and advisor to many startups.[5]

Here is what the SE Senior Manager at Oracle said:

> We were working with an IT director in re-
> placing some of their outdated hardware
> infrastructure with cloud infrastructure solu-
> tion. We had started on a few POC's (proof
> of concepts) and POVs (proof of values) with
> his team. We have engaged his team and they
> are putting a lot of time and effort into this.
> Eventually, the decision needs to be made by
> CIO to make the big purchase but without
> getting this group becoming our champion
> and making them look good, this will not be
> possible.

On the aspect of decision making, Paul Weinstein continues, "Champions are only one, crucial side of the deal
triangle—you also have to align the deal's blockers and
the decision makers. All three must be managed with
an understanding that people make decisions based on
personal and professional motivations that are often
hidden to the rest of the world. But once you get a
champion in your corner, you've made a major break-
through. You're ready to enter the ring."[5]

6. Find Your Champion and Industry Insider While Dealing with Gatekeepers

There is no doubt that C-suite executives seem like
the *be-all* and *end-all* for sales pitches. More power
and kudos to you if you can reach out to the highest
level of the decision-making chain of command during

any phase of the sales process. However, the reality for most salespeople is different. The most successful executives set strategy and vision, supply resources for their teams to execute this strategy and vision, and then get out of the way. Thus, a *champion* is essential to understanding the company's needs and providing guidance and advice on how to navigate the prospect's organization and their buying process. The role of this ally is to sell on your behalf when you're not there. They use all their power and influence to fight hard for your cause. Thus, one of the biggest challenges in the prospecting phase is learning how to spot a *champion*. Here are some characteristics of an effective champion:

1. They have a personal interest in driving your deal.
2. They have the power and influence to drive your deal.
3. They have a strong personality and know who to involve.
4. They are well known within their organization.[6]

Gatekeepers are key people who stand between you and the organization's upper management. They are often receptionists or administrative assistants whose job is to screen unwanted or irrelevant calls. You can also find higher ranking gatekeepers with substantial influence on the decision-making staff. The challenge is getting them in your corner. According to Lead Forensics, a B2B lead generating company, "To get past them, you simply need to convince them that talking to you will benefit the decision-maker. You need them to see that you're not just another jerk caller!" Here are some recommendations from Lead Forensics on interacting with gatekeepers:

1. **Be polite:** Try to engage with the gatekeeper on a personal level.
2. **Don't lie:** Be honest; give your full name, company name, and a brief overview of why you're calling.
3. **Build rapport:** As simple as it sounds, this can be one of the most powerful methods for getting through.
4. **Don't sell to the gatekeeper:** Don't try to pitch to the gatekeeper. They are unlikely to have any involvement in purchasing decisions.
5. **Use their knowledge:** Try to get them to share their knowledge with you. Ask them for their advice and insights, if possible. Listen to them carefully and make them feel valued.

7. Standing Apart From Competitors

During the prospecting stage, you're aiming to answer some key questions about your product. How is your product unique? In other words, concisely explain your position in the market and the value you offer customers. For example, Volvo positions itself as manufacturing the safest vehicle and Southwest Airlines sets itself apart by offering the lowest domestic fares. You must convey your company's and products' value by building trust, credibility, integrity, and the passion you demonstrate in each interaction with the prospect. The above are the key attributes of a *trusted advisor*, one whom the prospect can trust to find the right solutions to their challenges. In addition, as alluded to earlier (and will repeated again and again throughout this book), you can differentiate yourself from other sellers by actively listening to the prospect without judging or trying to jump in with a comment as soon as they pause. Try to listen empathetically to their challenges and understand where they want to be without passing judgment or telling them what they should and should not do.

At this early stage, with every customer interaction, you are representing your brand. Demonstrate your passion for helping them by being selfless and offering expert advice. As you will see later in the Presentation and Objection chapters, if your business isn't the best solution, be upfront and suggest better options. Showing that you have their best interests at heart is one of the best ways to stand apart from competitors. One semiconductor marketing executive—Mehdy Khotan, previously with Maxim—whom I interviewed offered these valuable insights: "This is very important, and it is the sales team's job to press marketing for it. Too many semiconductor companies struggle to make their differentiation crystal clear and quick to communicate." Tools used by marketing and sales teams include *fighting guides* and *SWOT* analysis. (SWOT stands for Strengths, Weaknesses, Opportunities, and Threats. Strengths and weaknesses are internal to your company—things that you have some control over and can change.) All the product positioning and competitive analysis are included in the fighting guide. In a nutshell, a fighting guide is a document that comprehensively compares and contrasts your products with the competition while identifying their position within the competitive landscape, which goes beyond publicly available information. They are filled with scripts and guidance on how to answer, refute, and address the prospect's questions and concerns. These tools are essential for sales teams to clearly and confidently demonstrate their value compared to the competition.

In the case of mounting competitive landscape, Hamid Karimi, vice president of Alliance and OEM at OPSWAT, a cybersecurity company, pointed out that, "Once an enterprise prospect becomes a customer, even after successful implementation, competitive pressure begins to build and, come renewal time, there is always a possibility of loss for the incumbent. It is uncommon to see renewal rates higher than 95 percent in enterprise sales."

8. Asking the Right Questions

While you might be tempted to make a pitch right away, don't. Rushing the process won't get you far. Instead, ask insightful and challenging questions to determine whether you can help your prospect and in what ways.

In asking the right questions, two schools of thought have developed over the years. *Solution Selling* versus *Insight Selling*.

According to the basics of *solution-selling*, the salesperson aligns a solution with an acknowledged customer need and then demonstrates why their offering is better than the competition's. Through general and specific questions, the salesperson can learn about the customer's needs and challenges. Then, the sellers can mold or attach their company's solutions to that problem.

The *insight selling* approach asserts that today's customer represents a radical departed from the old ways of buying, and sales leaders are increasingly finding that their staff is relegated to price-driven competition. These days, you may hear these words emanating from sales executives to encourage their reps to engage the customer much earlier, "Because the customers are coming to the table armed to the teeth with a deep understanding of their problem, it's turning many of our sales conversations into fulfillment conversations." That is, instead of asking customers to describe their needs, challenges, and the proverbial "what keeps them awake at night," they expect the salesperson—as the expert in the room—to have full insight into the industry and trends, to tell them what they should be worried about. For example, to begin the conversation, offer provocative insights about what the customer should do.[3] Moreover, today's customers embark on a "learning journey" when they set out to make a purchase, according to a 2017 Gartner Digital B2B Buyer Survey. The same survey revealed that 62 percent of that learning takes place outside of conversations with sellers.

Regardless of which strategy you choose, the sales team needs to be well-prepared. Avoid asking yes or no questions—you can do little with a one-word response. Instead, develop enough rapport so the prospect can share similar purchasing decisions they made in the past and their buying process. This information is priceless.

As explained in *Question that Sell* by Paul Cherry, asking an engaging question will not guarantee a positive outcome. Some prospects will not admit they need help; however, engaging and open questions will allow the salesperson to see the issues early on to determine the right course of action. A typical rookie mistake is asking three questions at a time without giving your prospect a chance to respond. *Expansion* questions allow you to sit back and let the customer do the talking. These questions develop the basic facts and lead to probing questions that elicit details.[1] For example, according to one executive of a business development company in the financial sector, one way to go about doing weeding out poor prospects is to use a simple tool like the *Concerns and Priorities* worksheet to uncover areas where you can offer solutions. By and large, probing, open-ended questions garner more information by encouraging the prospect to talk and elaborate on needs and vision. This will make the customer feel they are in control of the conversation. Be patient! You have to give the prospect time to consider one question at a time.

9. Staying Motivated

Although for some salespeople and managers the elusive number of likes, thumbs up, or followers on social media serve as motivators, they are not good indicators of success. According to Dr. Tino Alavi, CEO of Qvella, a medical device company in Ontario, Canada: "We strongly believe that Salespeople, more than other folks in your company, need to feel like they are winning. By their very nature, they are competitive."

Needless to say, sales representatives' motivation affects their productivity, the company's culture, and its bottom line. Hence, sales preparation includes setting goals for:

1. Contracting leads.
2. Identifying ideal candidates.
3. Outlining the expected outcome.

Accomplishing each of these goals is considered a small victory, which translates into even greater motivation. Without tangible and measurable goals, salespeople don't know what they are striving for.

Another important way to keep your team motivated is to invest in sales coaching. Sales training teams must empower sales managers to be better coaches, which subsequently helps boost motivation and sales performance for the entire team. So, here is what the earlier semiconductor marketing executive said on the motivation:

> Good salespeople do not like to waste their time and do not want to lose credibility with their customers. What motivates them is success. Success comes from good support, the follow-through to qualify the prospects, to make

sure what is promised to the customer is delivered on time, the products perform as they are promised, and knowing that their management or the marketing organization do not "leave them hanging" when a problem does occur.

10. Spending Too Much Time on Administrative Tasks

All the sales and marketing professionals, from the representatives to the vice presidents interviewed for this book, agreed this is a common, valid complaint from the sales team. That is, management wants to know what's going on in sales but doesn't have the right tools, which results in creating a lot of administrative work on the part of sales representatives. Particularly, since the start of COVID, which has turned all sales into inside sales, the need for good, easy to use, and transparent sales tracking tools has become urgent. More than ever, having a powerful and robust sales tool is a must not only to address the administrative sales tasks, but to capture all the previous customer interactions, feedback, etc. With all this information in a single location for all to see, collaboration within the sales team will come much easier.

In a 2018 article in *Forbes* magazine, Ken Krogue stated that today's salespeople are spending the majority of their time on activities other than sales. And here is the kicker:

Nearly two-thirds of salesperson's time, on average, is spent in non-revenue generating activities, leaving only 35 percent for functions related to selling. Administrative tasks like inputting data and generating reports eat up most of the sales reps' precious time.

So, in light of all the above challenges, experts believe that if certain customer relationship management (CRM) tool's functions can be improved to operate more seamlessly with other sales technology tools, sales teams would spend more productive time managing customer relationships, and in doing so, would see a measurable increase in sales because these sales tools and technologies can automate most non-revenue-generating tasks. With the right tools at their disposal, salespeople will have more time to devote to core activities and will be more motivated when they have the details of past customer interactions which will lead to future opportunities.[7]

11. Sales and Marketing: Not in Sync!

We have all heard of episodes when the CEO and marketing announce a product release way ahead of the actual release date when the new product is not even available for purchase. And if the product is available, it is full of bugs and defects. For experienced sales professionals, this seems like just another day in paradise. Just like many organizations or teams within a company, the sales and marketing teams—which seem to be joined at the hip—are often out of sync with each other. Miscommunication, incoherent sales and marketing campaigns, missed product lunch dates, etc. are all like egg on the face of a salesperson who always wants to present the right message, product, or services at exactly the right time.

Subsequently, prospects and/or potential customers feel betrayed, lied to, and uncertain. When this happens, no one can blame the prospect for going with another vendor or supplier, which has all its players rowing in the same direction. In many instances, the Oracle's senior sales manager said:

> As a sales engineer in few cases, I had to spend almost half the allotted time discussing what the marketing message meant and walk back some of the perceived promises, although my product was still superior to my competitors. But trying to explain the feature/functionality that was heard from marketing will be in a future release—well, that just took away some of the great highlights of my solution.

Although there is no silver bullet approach to the problem of miscommunication and delayed production, there are some obvious and proven recommendations to help alleviate the problem. Again, the same Oracle's manager continued:

> Marketing campaigns need to collaborate with the sales teams. I remember working with marketing on a campaign to invite prospects to a series of live roadshow style seminars. Marketing was mostly interested in putting butts in seats without paying attention to any targeted

industry or sales territory. These seminars resulted in attendance of over 400 people without producing any qualified leads. After these results, we regrouped and put together similar seminars but spent a week analyzing whom to target and from which industry while focusing on what geographic territories. As a result, these more focused seminars produced eight to ten high quality prospects, which resulted in building a substantial pipeline. And eventually, we were able to close many of them.

Of course, each industry and sales team faces many other challenges during the prospecting phases. According to the experts at ASLAN Training and Development, "Salespeople hate prospecting. Period. It has traditionally not been a fun part of the game. However, most of us who sell for a living know that we cannot have a robust pipeline if we don't prospect regularly."[8]

Thus, reach out to prospects for the first time either via email or voice mail to talk about a certain challenge or trend they are familiar with. If they are interested, they will certainly want to hear more. Remember, the immediate goal is to get to the next phase where you will discover and explore their specific needs to see whether this prospect represents a are real opportunity.

Summary:

In this chapter we learned:

1. Prospecting is the core, the foundation of every successful sales effort.

2. Having tons of leads is not always promising. Needless to say, you always want to keep the most qualified leads.
3. Don't compete with yourself by trying to pursue every possible lead and turn it into a prospect.
4. Create targeted prospecting using inbound and outbound strategies.
5. Identify and groom an internal champion to gain access and capture key decision-makers' attention.
6. Gatekeepers will always be between you the prospect; you need to deal with them professionally and confidently.
7. To get to the next round, salespeople must distinguish themselves from competitors by demonstrating the unique value of their products or services.
8. The success of solution selling or challenged sales strategies mainly depends on asking the right questions.
9. Research shows people look at business value first and then relationships.
10. Using a marketing automation platform, you can get automatic alerts so sales representatives are instantly notified when marketing passes them a lead.

Call2Action:

1. If you are new to sales (corporate or self-starting), take a class in the fundamentals of sales and marketing in addition to any sales training provided by your employer.
2. Find a sales mentor in the office or in your sales area.
3. Every quarter assess your own sales ability and seek feedback and mentorship from a senior peer or veteran salesperson on your wins and losses.
4. Watch the top performer(s) in your office and shadow them to see how they do it, why they are successful.

5. "Ride along" with senior or top performers during sales calls. If you can do this, it will be priceless.

6. Don't be afraid of rejection, mistakes, or failure while you find your unique selling style.

Bibliography:

[1]: *Questions That Sell: The Powerful Process for Discovering What Your Customer Wants*. Paul Cherry. AMACOM Publishing, 2006.

[2]: *Secrets of Question Based Selling*. Thomas A. Freese. Sourcebooks, 2003.

[3]: *The End of Solution Sales*. Brent Adamson, Matthew Dixon, and Nicholas Toman. *Harvard Business Review* July–August 2012.

[4]: *Target Marketing Systems*. Atlanta Georgia.

[5]: "To Close a Deal, Find a Champion." Paul Weinstein. *Harvard Business Review*. September 2014.

[6]: "How to Identify and Nurture a Sales Champion." Rizan Flenner. *iSEEit*, February 2016. https://now.iseeit.com/how-to-identify-a-meddic-champion/.

[7]: "Why Sales Reps Spend Less Than 36 Percent of Time Selling (and Less Than 18 percent In CRM)." Ken Krogue. *Forbes*. Jan 2018.

[8]: *The Number 1 Mistake Sales Reps Make When Prospecting*. Tom Stanfill. Aslan Sales Training Co.

CHAPTER 2

Initial Meeting: Discovery and Needs Recognition

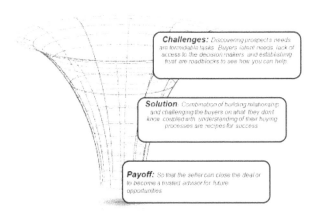

Challenges: Discovering prospect's needs are formidable tasks. Buyers latent needs, lack of access to the decision makers, and establishing trust are roadblocks to see how you can help.

Solution: Combination of building relationship and challenging the buyers on what they don't know coupled with understanding of their buying processes are recipes for success.

Payoff: So that the seller can close the deal or to become a trusted advisor for future opportunities.

In the previous chapter, I told you about my first sale. In that transaction, there was no need for an initial meeting nor a customer needs assessment. It just happened in the following sequence: the customer called, asked a couple of questions, and placed an order—bingo! Not many people wake up thinking they need a few hard disks and memory boards. My first customer may have been the only one. My first customer, the one who called out of the blue to place a substantial order—luckily right after learning how to take the order in the half-hour new-hire orientation—was a unicorn, a needle in a haystack, and sasquatch all rolled into one. If you look up beginner's luck, you'll find that transaction. After that one sale, like my colleagues, I had to hustle through prospecting by making endless cold calls—which to many of us was far less enjoyable than having our teeth pulled out.

Essential to Understand: Sales Roles vs. Account Management

For many of the sellers, it is a daily challenge to wear multiple hats throughout the sales transaction. However, in more enterprise-like (or B2B) purchases which often require good amount of relationship building between the sellers and buyers, it is important to distinguish between these two roles. Of course, each sales & marketing organization may have its own definitions and expectations; however, according to Dr. Andre Peine, the Head of Global Account Development and Excellence at Infineon Technologies, " a sales job is only to sell new and existing product offerings to a customer or to their sourcing/procurement departments." In general, this is the way most of the B2C sales (business-to-consumer sales model in which businesses target individual consumers) are performed. Whereas, in the account management, it is the sellers with all their internal resources from marketing, logistics, quality, development and top management that- in concert- need to interact with their peer entities on the customer's side throughout the sale process. Thus, these bi-directional communication and exchanges between your organization and your prospect's are essential for any successful deal closure in the realm of B2B selling.

Yet, Another Strategy: Inside-Out vs. Outside-in

In the previous chapter, identifying an effective and targeted prospecting strategy is always a challenge for the sales and marketing organizations. We showed the pros and cons of *inbound* and *outbound* strategies. Now, at the heel of initial meeting with your prospects to discover their needs, it is essential to point out these two business strategies of "*inside-out*" and "*outside-in*". In brief, an "inside-out" strategy is one that relies upon internal orientation and strengths in a couple of areas such as great technology, quality, great technical/customer service, affordable pricing, etc. Whereas with the "outside-in", according to Dr. Peine, "the approach is to better understand the needs of the customer and how we could generate additional value". Toyota and Appel are two examples for these two strategies. The former, which for decades has heavily relied on its great automotive technology and quality, tried to capture more market value by going head-to-head with GM (General Motors). This pushed Toyota to lose sight of customer needs and subsequently quality suffered. However, at Appel, the founder Steve Job, was able to address certain challenges and shortcomings at different time periods with iPod (condensing hundreds of high quality songs into a much smaller form factor than a CD player or music BOOM Box!); or later on, with the needs of being connected 24/7 to your emails while having mobile phone, photo, streaming, and on-line business services. In another words, subconscious to the customers, he masterfully conjugated the *why's*, *what's* and *how's* of all Apple's products to foster "the prospects' latent needs and translate them into solutions that will serve them."[1]

Having Your Initial Meeting Virtually

I was halfway through writing this book when the entire world was taken over by the COVID-19 pandemic. With all the human and economical carnage the coronavirus has created thus far—and more to come in the years ahead—the word *pandemic* was declared by Merriam-Webster Dictionary as the top word of the year 2020! As a result, B2B buying behavior has grown even more challenging, according to Gartner's report on the Future of Sales.[2] The report points to the digital sales channels acceleration over the next five years, when the number of digital (or virtual) interactions through video-conferencing between buyers and suppliers will skyrocket. Subsequently, sellers will face more challenges as the face-to-face interactions with their prospects or existing customers diminish. Although most of us are more comfortable interacting with our clients in person, we still need to discover their needs and their buying decisions remotely. Thus, Gartner's report strongly recommends sales organizations to invest on building more robust virtual customer engagement capability. This includes all the necessary presales call planning, preparation, and in-meeting practices for ensuring a productive and engaging dialogue with customers during virtual sales interactions. Therefore, going forward, many of the current or proverbial sales tasks and activities may also have these virtual and remote interaction components in them, which will add to the complexities and challenges in each phases of the sales process.

Basic Needs Analysis Questions

Now that you have successfully moved the prospect to the next step, the initial meeting, your main task is to discover and define their core needs accurately and succinctly. What you discover and gain from your prospects in this phase is the cornerstone to all the activities along the way in the sales process. During the first meeting, the discovery session, ask probing questions to identify the prospect's sense of urgency or scarcity. Here are some logical and plausible questions to ask prospects in this phase, as recommended by HubSpot, a leading software developer and marketer:[3]

1. What are your short-term goals? What are your long-term goals?
2. What are the risks if you don't address the current problems and/or challenges?
3. Who is your current vendor? Why did you choose them?
4. What do you like best about your present supplier? What don't you like?
5. What do you like best about your current system? What would you like to see changed?
6. What are your purchasing and success criteria?
7. Where would you rank price, quality, and service?
8. What will it take for us to do business?

Of course, we can come up with many more or derivatives of these essential questions. However, the challenge remains—you need an opportunity to ask them and a process for handling them that will move you to the next round. So, let's get to it.

From the Psychology of Buying

Throughout this book, I will repeat that buying is an emotional decision, and people do business with you because they know and trust you as a professional. Otherwise, they can easily go with someone else. For this to work, you must remain trustworthy and attentive to their needs. Although buying is emotional, it is justified and maintained logically. So, before you get hung up too much on the emotional roller coaster of selling, bear in mind that whether it's your sibling or a prospect you're selling to, they need to find value in your offering. And this is where the logical part of the brain comes into the picture. The consumer behavior model tells us that consumers ingest marketing and other stimuli, such as the four Ps: Product, Price, Place, and Promotion. The stimuli—either internal or external—enter their "buyer's black box" and then the "black box" creates their response.

Whether you're selling B2B (business-to-business) or B2C (business-to-consumer), the most logical phase of the sales process after prospecting is the initial meeting with the customer to discover their needs. B2B companies are support enterprises that offer goods and/or services other businesses need to operate and grow. For example, General Electric (GE) sells jet engines to Boeing for its 737 MAX planes, or ADP provides payroll services to many of the companies that sign your paychecks. This is in contrast to the business-to-consumer (B2C) model, which sells directly to individual customers. Take GE for example. Beyond jet engines, GE also sells washers and dryers to hotels and households through Best Buy or on its online stores. B2B companies have an entirely different target audience: They offer raw materials, finished parts, services, or consultation that other businesses need to operate, grow, and profit.[4] Regardless of which sales arena you are in, experts like the authors of *Mastering Technical Sales: The Sales Engineer's Handbook* have identified these three goals for the needs analysis and discovery stage:[5]

1. To increase your credibility with the customer,
2. To build your relationship and rapport with the customer, and
3. To develop an understanding of the problems faced by the customer.

Although we'll refer to the importance of credibility and rapport throughout the book, the focus of this chapter is the last goal—to improve the effectiveness and consistency of your needs analysis, which leads to a better understanding of the customer's needs.

Sales Receptivity

Today, prospects are bombarded with so much information from vendors at the speed of the internet, so you must have a clear and detailed understanding of their organizational challenges and become an agent of change, driving permanent improvements for the customer, according to Brett Clay in *Selling Change*.[6] But how can you do this? According to the experts at ASLAN, "When the prospect is guarded initially and emotionally 'closed,' you cannot persuade him/her with logical arguments. When attempting to persuade an emotionally closed person, he/she becomes even more closed." Therefore, the prospect's *receptivity* is more important to your ability to influence them than your product or service.

Gauging receptivity is the ability to read your prospect and determine whether they are keen to hear your message. Instead of regurgitating your product's features and benefits non-stop, be mindful that there is no value in talking when the prospect is not listening. That is, the content of your message is moot if they are not listening. Here are a few tips reaching indifferent prospects and creating an environment that fosters receptivity:

- *Drop the Rope:* The goal is to reduce the customary initial tension between the seller and buyer. If we eliminate the tension, we create more open conversations with honest, emotional answers that allow us to better serve prospects and create more and larger relationships.
- *Story Telling:* Yes! Convey past successes as a story. People love to hear stories similar to their own situation.
- *Emotions:* As we stated above, the emotional side of the brain does the buying and only checks in with the logical (or rational) side of the brain for affirmation. Many sellers tend to focus on satisfying the prospect's logical side with projections about ROI and other benefits of their products. While this is important, it is also essential to cater to the prospect's emotional side, to invite them to share their feelings, vision, and comfort that will come with a solution—hopefully, like the one you are offering them.

Problem recognition, when the prospect actually recognizes a problem or need, is the start of the buying process. Bear in mind that the prospect will not make a purchase as soon as they see a need. For example, you may be feeling hungry now, but you won't get up and drive to McDonald's to buy a hamburger!

All the sales and marketing experts concur that selling and buying are two sides of the same coin. That is, for any sales process there is also a buying process. Hence, it would pose a great challenge if a salesperson does not know the fundamentals of the buyer's purchasing process.

Defining the Purchasing Process:

The *purchasing process* is conducted by the consumer before, during, and after the purchase of products and services. The *buyer decision process* is usually split up into five distinct stages that typically occur in order:

1. Need Recognition
2. Information Search
3. Evaluation of Alternatives
4. Purchase Decision
5. Post-Purchase Behavior

This order seems to suggest that a consumer will pass through all five stages; however, this is not always the case. Often with habitual buying behavior, a consumer may skip or reverse some of these steps in the decision process. However, no one skips *need recognition*.

Also, during the pandemic, "B2B buyers increasingly want to engage with suppliers through digital and self-service channels. To support this shift to multi-experience buying, and the associated growth in the number of touchpoints and interactions between buyers and suppliers, sellers will need additional skills and technology capabilities," according to the same Gartner's study on the Future of Sales.[2] However, bear in mind that many sales situations in B2B are more complex than in B2C; that is, no single decision maker, and no pure focus on price apart from absolute commodities. Many products in B2B require explanations of their value proposition and cannot be covered using online and digital emporiums like Amazon or ebay, etc.

Need Recognition

In the Prospecting chapter, two strategies were pointed out; and it was the "outside-in" approach addresses the customers' needs more effectively. In general, need recognition refers to a consumer recognizing they have a need or problem that must be addressed. It is usually triggered by internal stimuli, such as hunger or thirst that rises to the level of an imperative. Conversely, external stimuli can create need too. For example, advertisements or word of mouth recommendations can lead consumers to consider buying a particular product. Of course, the above scientific facts have roots in the hierarchy of needs that the psychologist Abraham Maslow first described in 1943. He categorized all humans' needs into seven main divisions like: 1) physiological (water, air), 2) safety, 3) being loved, 4) esteem needs (achievements, prestige, and statues), 5) cognitive, 6) aesthetic (order, beauty, and structure), and 7) self-actualization and fulfillment. Based upon the above science, a study by Bain & Company shows how our elements of value approach extends those insights to people in corporate roles and their motivations for buying and using business products and services. The research went further with organizing 40 distinct kinds of value that B2B offerings provide potential customers into a pyramid with five levels. The most *objective* kinds of values such as "meeting specifications", "Acceptable price", "Economics", "Performance", "Regulatory compliance", and "Ethical standards" have been found at the *base* of the pyramid. And at the top of the pyramid, we can find more *subjective* and *personal* values. These so-called inspirational elements such as "Career", "Growth and Development", and "Reduced Anxiety" are those that will improve the customer's visions and hope for the future of the organization or the individual buyers.[7] Thus, by knowing more about the psychology of buying, you are in a much better position for an in-person meeting at the start of the discovery or needs analysis phase. During this phase, you will learn enough about your prospect to put together a personalized solution for them.

Also, it is more effective when prospects drive the conversation by expressing their needs; however, many experts like the authors of *The Challenger Sale* believe:

> Contrary to conventional wisdom, more traditional selling skills like needs analysis are much farther down the list when it comes to driving customer and influencer loyalty. So while organizations continue to pour time and money into helping reps to ask better more incisive questions, customers aren't looking for reps to anticipate, or discover, needs they already know they have, but rather to teach them about opportunities to make or save money that they didn't even know were possible.[8]

Also, despite the prospect's willingness to talk to you in person in the initial meeting phase, you may see some resistance getting them to open up so you can better address their needs. Inherently, potential buyers are emotionally closed, as you will see in the Qualification module, so we will cover how to read between the lines during conversations with potential customers and what types of questions can help you gather the insights you need. But prior to asking insight-gathering questions, you must set the stage and prime the client for those questions.

So, let's sum up this section on a quote by Henry Ford which illustrates the importance of challenger sale and the "outside-in" approaches, "if I had asked people what they wanted, they would have said *faster horses!*"

What Are the Challenges?

The decades old question organizations ask is: between sales and marketing, who should perform the needs recognition, analysis, and diagnosis? The jury is still out on this, and we are not going to spend time debating which is correct and why. The important thing is this: identifying the challenges salespeople will face chasing executives to get an initial meeting. Studies by Target Marketing Systems (TMS) showed that 85 percent of executives usually or always got involved in purchase decisions early in the buying cycle when they:

- Needed to understand current business issues.
- Established project objectives.
- Set overall project strategy.

Adding to the above mix, remembering some of the challenges from the previous chapter, most customers today have done their homework and are equipped with information on the solutions and offering they seek.

Nevertheless, executives tend to reduce their involvement during the evaluation phase of a project, delegating decisions to subordinates or committees. Eighty percent never or occasionally involve themselves in the middle of the purchase cycle, including:

- Exploring options
- Setting criteria for evaluating vendors
- Examining alternative solutions

For activities that occur late in the purchase decisions cycle, over half of senior executives are involved in:[9]

- Planning the implementation of the project.
- Supervising the measurement of project results.

For example, some believe the executive's involvement should be in the final stages to bless the decision or negotiate the final price. In short, most senior executives become involved in key purchasing decisions early, are less involved in the middle, and reassert themselves at the end of the buying process. Because senior executives are concerned with their organization's business needs, they are most likely to meet with a salesperson early in a sales cycle to assess the potential business value of the proposed sale. The Toronto-based medical device company CEO pointed to the financial effect of the sale. According to him, "It is not the purchase but rather the impact it might make on existing workflow."

Thus, to gain a spot on the prospect's calendar, you must show that a meeting will provide valuable information and an outline of the payoff likely with your offering.

In chapter four, we cover presentation techniques and best practices to help convey your key points more effectively. However, when communicating this information, a common landmine many sellers step on is selling an impossible future or promising the moon. A lot of salespeople see product roadmap data and either explicitly or implicitly sell based on unexecuted plans. Often, companies change plans or fail to deliver on time, which undermines the salesperson's credibility.

How Can Salespeople Gain High-Level Access?

The most common reasons executives take a meeting:

- Existing relationship
- Company reputation
- Product/Service
- Internal referral
- Strategic vendor

Of the methods employed by salespeople to gain an audience with senior executives, studies have shown that cold calls are least successful. For example, in a survey by the TMS group, 80 percent of respondents said they would never or only occasionally meet with salespeople making cold calls. Moreover, a letter or an email sent before a call is not likely to improve the odds of meeting either.[9]

Focusing on two of the above reasons like existing relationships and internal referrals, we can learn a lot from the experience of Qvella's CEO in Toronto, Canada. According to him, "It is widely recognized that the key to making an initial technical sale is an internal champion. But the challenge is how to find this internal champion." He continues, "Not all champions are empowered equally. Some are diehard technology enthusiasts with little purchasing power. So how do you find your champion effectively?"

We described the roles and importance of a champion in the previous chapter. For example, for years, his medical device company wanted to penetrate key hospitals and medical research facilities in the US. However, they had not been successful.

> We hired the clinical laboratory director of the largest not-for-profit HMO (Health Maintenance Organization) in the US to help guide our strategy. As a well-known industry veteran, she works as a trusted medical/clinical advisor to our potential customers. The key is that she's not seen as part of our sales team! In this vein, she fulfills two purposes: 1) she helps identify internal champions (she has a great reputation and vast experience, so people respect and respond to her), in other words, she helps to open the door, 2) she helps to sort out technical/clinical issues as they come up, in other words, she provides after-sales support.

More than half of the executives interviewed in the same TMS Group survey prefer inhouse introductions to salespeople rather than outside referrals. Also, about 84 percent of those interviewed indicated they would usually or always grant a meeting with a salesperson based on a recommendation from inside their firm. In the previous chapter, we talked about the significant services that an inside champion can provide. However, it is important to make sure the *champion* does not feel the seller is trying to go over their head. That is, the seller has to build a lot of trust with the champion.

Once you build trust, the champion will tell you when it's the best time to get executives involved. If you are dealing with a *gatekeeper* rather than a champion, the seller has to negotiate for access in a *quid pro quo* process. Also, as alluded to in the previous chapter, an inside champion is essential to opening doors and guiding you toward executive access.

You also need to make the champion's job easier and make them look good by providing information on the latest updates, features, and insights to the extent that your management allows you to share information. One way to enhance the relationship and highlight the champion is through social selling, which helps make the connection with executives via shared contacts. Try to elevate your company and your champion's visibility by providing testimonials from people who have trusted your champion in the past.

What Roadblocks Do Executives Use To Screen Salespeople?

By in large, executives employ a variety of methods to screen, test, and block salespeople. Having administrative assistants filter calls and email, sticking to schedules/priorities, and delegating incoming requests to a subordinate are common blocking methods.

If you get passed the first hurdle, you will be tested quickly. Most respondents to the TMS survey said cold-calling salespeople get five minutes to show how they can add value. In an initial contact, the four primary methods used to persuade a senior executive you can add value are:[9]

- Focus on the business perspective and don't get caught up in the bells and whistles of the product.
- Raise relevant questions and share new perspectives with the executive.
- Point out the potential limitations of your products or services, thus enhancing your credibility.
- Ensure your discussion is less scripted and show authenticity.

Executives use the first meeting to answer these specific questions:

1. Does the salesperson understand our needs? Have they done their homework (i.e. do they understand our industry, our strategies)? Do they understand our key business drivers?
2. Have they been able to convey how their product/service applies to us? Why is it better than its competitors?
3. Is this individual an empowered decision-maker, or will they have to consult their sales manager before making decisions?
4. Is the salesperson's approach:
    a. Professional?
    b. Confident?
    c. Sharp (thinks on their feet, doesn't use a canned speech)?

d. Honest (acknowledges potential shortcomings)?
e. Reflective (listens more than talks)?
f. Flexible (has an unstructured agenda rather than a predetermined one)?

How Do Salespeople Make Meeting Effective?

To better understand executives' perceptions of initial sales meetings and the challenges salespeople face, the Target Marketing Systems, Inc. survey identified two leading criteria in gauging the effectiveness of a first interaction: (1) the ability to demonstrate accountability and responsibility, and (2) the ability to demonstrate an understanding of the customer's business goals, objectives, and challenges. Other effective behaviors included good listening skills, industry expertise, and knowledge of the given business.

Interestingly, a salesperson as a "source of information about competitors," gleaned less than three out of five. The majority of executives said their trust is eroded if a salesperson reveals information about competitors. "If they do it to them, they could do it to us!"

It is essential to make initial meetings effective so the buyer returns for the next phase. As the VP of Alliance & OEM at the cybersecurity firm OPSWAT points out, "Sometimes the first meeting becomes either an opportunity for the sales teams to show off or to derail the conversation. Unless asked, salespeople should never bash competitors. And last, they should have a call-to-action plan and not abdicate by completing the meeting without knowing the next step."

How Do Salespeople Establish Trust and Credibility With Executives?

Executives rated a salesperson's ability to marshal resources from within the salesperson's organization as the most important factor in building a trusted advisor relationship. This often includes a set of compelling insights that you, as a trusted advisor, can teach your customers—something new and valuable about how to compete in the customer's market. Remember, it is not just your product and/or services you are selling, it is the insight you deliver as part of the sales interaction.[8]

Executives also gave high marks to a salesperson's understanding of the customer's business goals, objectives, and challenges. Other highly rated factors include "responsiveness to [the customer's] requests" and demonstrating a "willingness to be held accountable."

One common myth is that you should always send someone with many years of experience to meet with potential customers, or that inexperienced salespeople cannot interact well with an executive. Here's the thing—the lowest rated criterion was a salesperson's length of service. Executives valued decisiveness and confidence more than years of service in salespeople. One contributing vice president told us they appreciate a salesperson who "speaks with authority but without arrogance."

Going back to what was mentioned in the previous chapter, rather than living by the rule *always be closing* (ABC, which became very popular after the hit movie *Glen Gary, Glen Ross*), you should instead aim for ABH (always be helping). If you're contacting a business that's a good fit and can genuinely benefit from your product or service, then you're being helpful. If you sound nervous or stressed, you'll immediately be giving off warning signals. Stay relaxed, speak calmly and authoritatively, and give only as much information as you need to.

Moreover, the executives interviewed for this book were most impressed by salespeople who express genuine interest in their customers' buying needs, who are knowledgeable about their industry, and who think strategically. High-ranking executives also prefer salespeople who are responsive and who listen more than they talk.

Here is an observation from the engineering senior manager at Oracle about the art of selling and listening:

> Salespeople go into a meeting wanting to give pricing and start negotiating at this early stage. You can't talk about cost and pricing too early. Customers sometimes just want to be educated or they are just kicking the tires. I have heard buyers say, "I have not even told you my needs and you are giving me a price! It's more about what you are selling than what I need," as many potential customers have complained as a turn off by many sellers. Also, bad-mouthing competitors is another thing, particularly if you don't know people's allegiances. As a rule of thumb, listen 80 percent of the time and talk 20 percent. Always act as an educator rather than a pushy sales rep.

In addition, executives are much more likely to remember a bad sales meeting than a good one. Negative perceptions come from negative practices such as lack of focus, ignoring details, being a know it all, and pushing products rather than meeting the customer's needs. Often, so much time and energy are wasted enumerating features, the prospect gets bored and inattentive.

RFP (Request for Proposal)

In some cases, like with larger companies, government agencies, and other public sector prospects, a request for proposal (RFP) will be issued to vendors and suppliers with the intention of gathering information on potential suppliers' companies, products, and solutions. These large companies and public entities want you to fill out these long forms—ten to a hundred pages—thoroughly. RFPs tell you that you are dealing with a prospect that knows exactly what they want and have experience with the process.

Regardless of whether this it is a simple proposal or an in-depth RFP, it is typically the weakest point in the sales process for most vendors. Why is this? After all, a proposal is essentially the vehicle for a vendor's offerings, and if executed ineffectively, it can render an entire sales process null up to the proposal submission. Your product or offering could truly be the right choice for the buyer, but if your proposal doesn't convey your product/service's value and articulate your uniqueness and superiority, you will likely lose the business.

Below are four challenges associated with proposal and RFP generation, and how they can be tackled according to Seismic, a leading sales enablement company:

Challenge #1: Efficiently crafting a customized story

Simply put, your proposal must be customer-centric. It must articulate the customer's need and how your solution will uniquely address the why, what, and how within a certain time scope. RFPs and proposals are often on strict deadlines, and you never know how many of these proposals their teams will have at a time.

Challenge #2: Empowering sellers to take on proposals independently

Most organizations have a proposal team or at least an individual dedicated to completing proposals. But this doesn't mean the sales team can't help, too.

Challenge #3: Sifting through all existing RFPs and proposals for appropriate responses. Most proposal teams have a file folder of all completed and submitted RFPs, and spend time locating past answers. This is time-consuming and risky, considering answers may be outdated or geared to a specific buyer and may not be appropriate for the current proposal. As touched upon in the first challenge, having a knowledge base of existing RFP questions is imperative to efficiently and thoughtfully crafting a proposal.

Challenge #4: Rounding up subject matter experts to provide the best responses

The best RFPs incorporate knowledge from individuals across the vendor's entire organization.

Of course, none of these challenges can be addressed without a proper content management software tool or system along with a defined process. Silos must be broken down, sales, marketing, and proposal teams must be centered on collaboration and efficient workflows, and companies must be dedicated to diligently managing content (including RFPs and response knowledge bases). This preparation results in shorter sales cycles, higher win rates, and more closed deals. **[10]**

Successful discovery and need analysis hinge on a non-interrogational but conversational discovery session to get some honest information from your prospect. Instead of being self-centered and trying to sell after a few minutes of conversation, first focus on the problem the prospect is trying to solve. From there, reserve talk about solutions until you have a complete understanding of the problem.

Summary

Here is what we discussed in this chapter:

1. If your company is on the shortlist of the vendors or suppliers, you will be permitted to ask questions of the prospect.
2. Via RFPs, sellers can do a needs analysis, diagnosis problems, and create a solution with the buyer.
3. It is known that we tend to buy from people who validate our pain and current challenges.
4. Executives tend to take meetings with salespeople who are referred by an internal champion.

5. These champions are often industry veterans, experts, or industry insider who can open doors and act as a trusted advisor.
6. The use of an internal or external trusted advisor can effectively help you extract much-needed information when your line of questioning starts with, "*Because you have told us....*"
7. Typical landmines in this phase include getting into feature selling before the buyer has even explained the problem.

Call2Action:

1. Know your product or service beyond what's on the sell sheets.
2. If you internalize these ideas, please pay it forward.

Bibliography:

[1]: "The B2B Elements of Value," by Eric Almquist, Jamie Cleghorn, and Lori Shere, *Harvard Business Review*, March-April 2018.
[2]: "The Future of Sales, Transformational Strategies for B2B Sales Organizations," 2020, Gartner Inc.
[3] *Sales Questions to Ask a Customer to Determine Their Needs.* Tony Alessandra. HubSpot.
[4]: "What Is B2B?" Adam Uzialko. *Business News Daily.* June 2020.
[5]: *Mastering Technical Sales: The Sales Engineer's Handbook/* 3rd ed. John Care and Aron Bohlig. ARTECH House, 2014.
[6]: *Selling Change.* Brett Clay. Aviva Publishing, 2010.

[7]: "The B2B Elements of Value," by Eric Almquist, Jamie Cleghorn, and Lori Shere, *Harvard Business Review*, March-April 2018.

[8]: *The Challenger Sale*. Matthew Dixon and Brent Adamson. Portfolio/Penguin, 2011.

[9]: "Selling to Senior Executives," by Target Marketing Systems [TMS].

[10]: "4 Major Challenges of Proposal and RFP Generation." Alyssa Drury. *Seismic*. Nov 2016.

CHAPTER 3

Qualification Phase

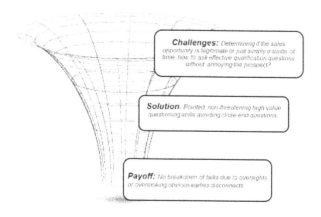

Challenges: Determining if the sales opportunity is legitimate or just simply a waste of time, how to ask effective qualification questions without annoying the prospect?

Solution: Pointed, non-threatening high value questioning while avoiding close-end questions.

Payoff: No breakdown of talks due to oversights or overlooking obvious earlier disconnects.

It would be great if all of sales questions lead to prospects asking, "When do we start?" or "Where should I sign?" However, to our dismay, that's not usually the case. It would also be nice if prospects had infinite budgets and authority to sign purchase orders after asking a few questions of the salesperson. Unfortunately, nothing in life falls into our laps as soon as we request it. That is why we've covered the numerous challenges and the dos and don'ts of sales during the prospecting and needs recognition phases. If you have made it to this stage, job well done. As a reward, you will learn about another series of challenges and problems in the next phases—starting with qualifying your prospects.

Why Wait? They Are Interested and Ready to Buy?

Well not so fast. Even though the person you've talked to has expressed fervent interest and is very keen to buy your product, you have to thoroughly vet potential customers, their organization, and the deal in general. As pointed out in the introduction, as one of the steppingstones to a successful closing, *Qualifying* means determining if the sales opportunity is legitimate. The main challenge in this phase is figuring out how to funnel the customer. You use qualification questions to do so. You may ask why?

As a salesperson, you need to be mindful of people who are not always forthright with their answers. Because, often, as described in the book *Question That Sell* by Paul Cherry, "Prospects are afraid to say no, or they don't trust salespeople, or they anticipate possible problems down the road with their current vendor and want to keep their options open, or they are not even aware that there is a problem or need."[1] Therefore, not many salespeople feel comfortable asking qualification questions. As a result, you either encounter objections in future phases of the sales process, or painfully, you may have to walk away from the deal. Similarly, many potential customers may be offended by qualifying questions such as: 1) Are you the decision-maker? 2) Do you have budget and funds approval for this deal? 3) How committed are you to going forward with this purchase?

In the prospecting chapter, you did pre-qualification with cold calls, cold email, and networking at conferences or conventions. And as a result of those activities, you've elevated your leads to prospects and then to potential customers worth your and their time. Remember, back then you were not asking them to purchase anything—you were merely exploring. Soft, probing, pre-qualifying questions looked at 1) needs, 2) reasons to change, 3) affordability, or 4) is there an interest or value? These were all meant to determine if it made sense and would be mutually beneficial to continue the conversation.

Going Down the Path of Qualification

Of course, not every lead is a good fit for a product or service—no matter how strongly a salesperson believes they are (or wants them to be). On the flip side of the coin, the book *Always Be Qualifying* reminds us that, "Successful sellers are those who spend their time prospecting [those] who will end up buying."[2]

Also, we know by now that buyers don't buy just because they have a serious need or a looming deadline or money to burn. They buy because of a combination of all of these factors and more. As stated in the previous chapter, we buy emotionally, and back our decision with logic and reason. During sales qualification, salespeople must establish fit based on as many of these criteria as possible. They establish fit based on all relevant factors.

Throughout this chapter, we discuss the various challenges in this round based on the fundamental criteria depicted in Figure 4's enhanced flowchart, based on the idea originated by the Lucidchart, which provides designs for anything from brainstorming to project management.

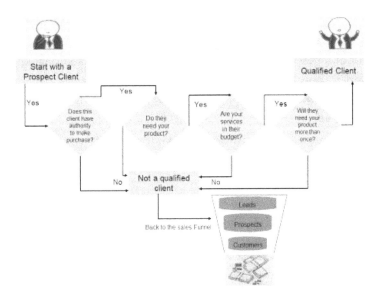

Figure 4.

Of course, every industry is different; however, you can funnel your potential customers by asking them questions around four criteria which are the same for all potential customers. These four questions are formally known as *BANT* which stands for *Budget, Authority, Need,* and *Time.* However, BANT's efficacy in the modern selling environment is debatable. For example, buyers don't have pre-defined projects with set budgets and timelines anymore. And asking sales representatives to BANT qualify every lead that comes their way means they probably won't get a lot of leads.

Others have defined a new lead qualification methodology. This methodology is the *ANUM* model which stands for *Authority, Need, Urgency,* and *Money.* The difference in this model is that:

> ANUM proposes to create demand higher within the prospect organization against project-based selling. Sales reps with the help of marketing must build need with authority figures, create an urgency to purchase, and then help them figure out how they are going to fund it.[3]

However, another methodology or criterion determining whether or not you should expend effort getting a customer into your sales funnel is MEDDIC. The author and executive sales coach Darius Lahoutifard believes that, "MEDDIC is the most renowned sales qualification methodology, applicable to any enterprise sales process, which is inherently complex." Its definition is composed of six elements:

- **METRICS**: Measure the potential gain leading to the economic benefit of your solution versus the competition.
- **ECONOMIC BUYER**: Identify and meet the person who has the ultimate authority to release funds to purchase.
- **DECISION PROCESS**: Know and influence the process defined by the client to make purchasing decisions.
- **DECISION CRITERIA**: Know and influence the criteria defined by the client to make purchasing decisions.
- **IDENTIFY PAIN**: Identify and analyze the pain which require your solution to be relieved.
- **CHAMPION**: Identify, qualify, develop, and test your champion or internal seller.

In some respects, MEDDIC contradicts BANT. One of the primary promises of MEDDIC is to transform the urgency of sales into urgency to save costs or to increase revenue. Thus, it is certainly a challenge for sales teams to select the right approach to qualifying prospects. For example, you may use BANT for less complex, more transactional deals which have a shorter sales cycle. But you need to consider MEDDIC for enterprise opportunities.

Interrogator vs. Trusted Advisor

Trust is one of the main pillars of a successful buying journey and starts with the strength of your product or service. So, regardless of your organization's method for qualifying prospects, the process is challenging. Traditionally, sellers have stated that it is often daunting to get straightforward answers from potential customers about sensitive information like budgeting, authority, timing, etc. In another words, most buyers in the early stages of purchasing tend to keep information regarding their challenges, needs, and resources, or lack of these, close to the vest. In these situations, experts strongly suggest exercising *receptivity*—which we outlined in the previous chapter—to ask qualifying questions in a non-threatening manner.

This is not only limited to the qualification phase, but continues throughout the entire sales cycle—as a trusted advisor all your questions must be prepared and asked with the sole intention of helping clients overcome challenges. You must set the stage before asking sensitive questions. In another words, priming the prospect is very crucial to extracting key information.

For example, consider the gist of the following private conversation between John Chambers, the former CEO of Cisco Systems, and Bob LaFort, the president of Infineon Technologies, on the issue of cybersecurity. Chambers alluded to there being two types of companies: those that have been hacked, and those that don't know they've been hacked. Obviously, if you are pursuing an IT security opportunity, the prospect will not volunteer that their infrastructure had been compromised— let alone going into details about their infrastructure security failures. If you were the potential prospect, would you willingly talk to a sales representative you hardly know about those horrible corporate experiences? Most likely not.

Effectively, you are walking a fine line between interrogator and trusted advisor. We also defined the roles of a trusted advisor in the previous chapter. From a respected expert to an industry insider, trusted advisors mainly educate and consult, offering advice and various options. As Qvella's CEO said, "Having a trusted advisor removes friction from the sales process." Having a trusted advisor significantly removes friction from the sales process

At the same time, your main goal is eliciting the guiding clues needed to move the deal forward. Remember, you need to qualify for all four characteristics, but you don't need to do them in a particular order. You should change your approach to fit the prospect's convenience.[4]

Again, I emphasize that budget, money, authority, timeline, and need are the most important criteria you need to qualify your prospect against. This makes sense, given that deals can't go forward without these elements. However, this approach may be misconstrued as uncaring by the prospect. That is why the salesperson should also tailor their qualifying questions to the customer's plans, challenges, and the potential consequences of the deal falling through, so salespeople can get much deeper into the prospect's strategy and help them rethink what's possible.[5]

Reading Between the Lines When Receiving Responses to High-Value Questions

As mentioned earlier, one of the main challenges is to come up with qualifying questions that will not be misconstrued as disrespectful or suspicious and yet, eliciting responses that ultimately provide clues and insight about the prospect's current situation. But before we describe the different types of questions, as you read in the previous section, to obtain more useful answers, you must prime your prospects before asking probing questions. Yes, you can always start with "tell me…" or "how do you…" or "explain to me..." etc. However, the answers may be terse at best. Whereas, if you start with "because you told us…." qualifying questions, the prospect will know you were actively listening when they described their problem. Now that you're quoting something from their playbook, they are more willing to share the information you need.

Short, *closed-ended* questions often end conversations (i.e.: yes, no, always, sometimes, never, etc.). They are the most detrimental way to qualify potential customers. Often, salespeople think this is the most pointed and effective way to cut to the chase—but then see that the conversation ends abruptly, without providing any valuable information to move the deal forward.

On the other hand, *a high-value* question during this stage is one that creates a learning experience for both you and the prospect; it provides the needed insights to move the conversation forward. More importantly, these questions—and their follow ups—will help you gain the trust and credibility you are after.

High-value questions are mainly *open-ended*. Start with an open question which allows the potential customer to feel they are in control. Open-ended questions facilitate a conversation because they can't be answered with one word. An example of an open-ended question would be "Where do you want to be in five years?" Of course, the answer varies from person to person. For example, if the prospect is neither engaged nor ready, they might just say, "I'm not sure" or "hard to say" or "it depends" or any similar terse answer, which generally bring the conversation to the end.

In contrast, if your initial pitch and message have been effective, the above questions can be answered with a unique perspective that usually prompts a longer conversation. Here's some more examples of open-ended questions:

- How would you describe your current situation related to your supplier?
- Why are you after opportunities in this market segment?
- How would you measure your success after adopting a new learning management tool?
- What are the consequences of not updating your corporate network infrastructure?

By and large, open-ended questions prompt longer conversations by asking questions starting with *why, how,* and *what if?* Also, to help you craft better questions, *Always Be Qualifying* suggests the *T-H-E-D* method. This stands for:[2]

- "Tell me about…."
- "How do you…."
- "Explain your…."
- "Describe your…."

As you can imagine, the above questions allow the prospect to expand and give more detailed answers. It is better to stays away from *closed-ended* questions which can be answered with a single word, such as yes or no. Of course, *open-ended* questions and *closed-ended* questions both have their place in sales conversations. For example, if you're only looking for short or quantitative answers, like the number of accounts the prospect's company has, the company's annual revenue, or their desired daily output, then asking a closed-ended question is appropriate. But when it comes to learning qualitative information during initial discovery, open-ended questions can go a long way.

Converting From Close-Ended to Open-Ended Questions

At a certain point during your lengthy question and answer session, both you and your prospect eventually only want to hear *yes, no, never, always, maybe.* As a result, the subsequent challenge would be how to follow up on a closed-ended question with an open-ended one? For example, when you ask a potential prospect—who at the moment does not fully need your offerings—if they are happy with their current training provider, the conversation will end on this three-letters word answer, yes. What would you say next? How would you salvage the conversation? In this case, either rephrase your initial question or follow it up with, "If yes, can you describe their content development and delivery process?"

In general, open-ended questions are designed to start conversations. You shouldn't be surprised or thrown off if the answers lead to tangents. Therefore, in addition to situational fluency, you should have a plan for mining tangential answers for useful information, and be happy because it means your open-ended questions were successful.[6]

Summary:

The following key points were discussed in this chapter:

1. Sales qualification is the part of the sales process in which you determine whether a prospect is a good fit for the product or service you are selling.
2. Sales qualification is the answer to the question, "How do you determine if a prospect is a good fit for your product or service?"
3. Questioning the prospect on their BANT may not sit well with them.
4. BANT and MEDDIC are the two most common methodologies for qualifying prospects.
5. BANT should be used for small, transactional deals with short sales cycles.

6. MEDDIC approach is for more complex, enterprise deals which encompass a longer sales cycle.
7. Prior to asking high-value questions, make sure you prime the customer by setting the stage and telling the prospect why you need to know so they don't block your questions mentally.
8. Make sure you're actively listening to help build rapport with prospects and become one of their trusted advisers.
9. By developing a joint strategy for qualifying leads, your sales team can improve its ability to focus on good leads.
10. Qualification should be a constant activity throughout the sales process to avoid wasting time and potential opportunities.
11. Better qualification means more sales, faster closing, and full-price deals.

Call2Action:

1. Familiarize yourself with corporate financial statements which are often used to financially vet potential buyers.
2. What are some of qualification questions your management team would like you to ask prospects?
3. Study and gain more insight into the MEDDIC methodology and philosophy by visiting their website.

Bibliography:

[1]: *Questions That Sell, The Powerful Process for Discovering What Your Customer Really Wants*. Paul Cherry. AMACOM Publishing, 2006.

[2]: *Always Be Qualifying*, Darius Lahoutifard, 01 Consulting, July 2020.

[3]: *14 Lead Qualification Questions to Spot "Sales-Ready" Leads*. Francis Cyriac, *Inside Sales Box* and Ken Krogue of *Forbes* magazine.

[4]: "How to Use BANT to Qualify Prospects in 2020." Aja Frost. Hubsport.com.

[5]: "Sales Qualification Improves Close Rates." Pete Caputa. Hubspot.com.

[6]: "The Art of Asking Open-Ended Questions." Bill Cates. Hubspot.com.

CHAPTER 4

The Art of Presenting Your Solution

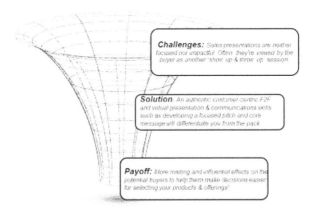

Challenges: Sales presentations are neither focused nor impactful. Often they're viewed by the buyer as another 'show up & throw up' session

Solution: An authentic, customer-centric F2F and virtual presentation & communications skills such as developing a focused pitch and core message will differentiate you from the pack

Payoff: More riveting and influential effects on the potential buyers to help them make decisions easier for selecting your products & offerings'

So, this is it! "Showtime!" Congratulations! Now, whether under the same roof or virtually, you have to bring your "A" game to the potential buyer and stakeholders to take advantage of this golden opportunity to showcase your product or offering. Although you are excited to talk about your offering's features, benefits, and advantages, the potential buyer mainly wants to hear about the services, quality, price, and, above all, the ROI they would receive from your product.

Receiving an invitation from the potential buyer to present or demonstrate to their stakeholders shows you are interacting with a qualified and committed customer who has authority, an allocated budget, and most importantly, the need for your solution or product offering. So, job well done thus far! As you recall from the prospecting chapter, the salesperson's immediate goal is always to maintain the conversation and relationship to get to the next phase of the sales process. So here you are on the next round of engagement with your potential customer.

I always remind our sales and technical staff of this quote by Dale Carnegie, author and pioneer in the field of public speaking: "There are always three speeches, for every one you actually gave: 1) The one you practiced, 2) the one you gave, and 3) the one you wish you gave."

Problem, Solution, and Payoff Framework as Part of Sales Enablement

In my current role as the sales enablement training manager, my main focus is to elevate the presentation skills of our technical subject matter experts (SMEs). Although our technical sales and marketing colleagues walk on water when it comes to technical expertise, when selling or promoting many of them tend to revert to their comfort zones of heavily pitching features and benefits from start to finish. During my coaching sessions with them, I place a heavy emphasis on presenting ideas, products, or any offerings by using the *problem, solution, payoff* framework. In fact, outside of the sales and marketing arena, we constantly see politicians, environmentalists, and advertisers regularly use this framework to grab their audience's attention quickly to promote their policies, ideas and products. One of the six principles that an idea will stick to the mind of your audience is *unexpected danger*, according to the Heath brothers in their bestselling book, *Made to Stick*.[1] The authors claim, "For any potential buyer, you want to convey this message that by not acting on your advice or not investing in your product or offering could harm their business and pose a danger to compete successfully." Also, the other main principles mentioned in this book are *credibility, emotion,* and *stories.*

It is quite a challenge for some presenters with a purely technical background to put on a business hat to influence or promote a sale; because of this, our team at the Sales & Marketing Academy (SaMA) of Infineon coaches our technical subject matter experts (SME) during training workshops on various best practices of presentation, such as content development, delivery styles, and handling Q&A during and after their talks. One key factor of successful presentations is to have a *strong opening* and a *strong closing*. To achieve this, we make our presenters mindful that opening and closing matter the most. Why? Because, as shown in the attention curve depicted in Figure 5, whether it's with a speech, book, or movie, research shows that the audience's attention is at its peak during the first and last parts and then ebbs in the middle of due to constant distractions from things like cell phones, email, and social media.

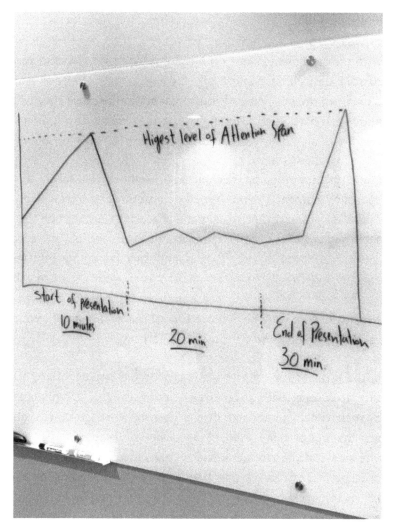

Figure 5.

Therefore, always make sure you start by showing confidence and credibility as soon as you take the stage. By starting with, "Because you've told us about your current problems...." you will show you understand their current challenges. And by continuing with "That's why we recommend (products, steps, processes, etc.) as a solution to your…." This opening, along with the statements like, "With this approach, we can take you to your desired destination of…," will gain their attention and trust from the beginning of your presentation because they will know you have been listening to them earnestly and have arrived with an exclusive solution or remedy for their problem.

Many salespeople or technical presenters consider this approach elementary and they take these three powerful statements for granted; thus, making the precarious assumption that their audience fully understands the purpose and objective of the presentation. By not clearly and succulently stating the *problem, solution*, and *payoff* statements early, your audience will not be able to follow your presentation effectively. To be effective, make sure they hear these crucial points along with your recommendation and core message early on.

In the prospecting chapter, we identified the challenges of getting a meeting with executives—first getting a few minutes of their time, and second, delivering your message when you get the opportunity. Well, in *Speaking Up*, Frederick Gilbert interviews distinguished industry executives, asking how to present to executives. The late Dan Eilers (managing director at Vanguard and former CMO at Appel) said, "If you want executives to be part of your deal, you're going to [have to] engage them; but you have to engage them quickly. Successful presenters will get to the point immediately."[2]

The odds of holding an executive's attention are slim. According to a study by Insidesales.com (now Xant, a sales engagement company), only 15 to 20 percent of CIOs and other executives find sales presentations valuable. But only 6 percent would go to another meeting with the presenter. Why?

1. The presentation was not informative enough.
2. The presentation did not come across as consulting.
3. The presentation did not identify the product/service's added value.

That's why we mentioned at the beginning of this chapter that you must bring your A game to presentations. You have to be fully prepared mentally and technically to present yourself as authentically as possible while setting yourself apart by knowing your product's strengths and weaknesses. These challenges present a strong headwind that grows even stronger when you have to present remotely/virtually. (We'll cover this later in the chapter.)

You will win or lose with the first slide—your position must be clear from the start. Remember, you are not going to get their business by just expressing your understanding of their problem. You must also need to show them you can lead them to their desired destination successfully. That is why you need to state your main points and recommendations—something that can't be rebuffed—early on so you can gain and retain their attention through the rest of your presentation.

Proving Yourself as a Trusted Advisor:

You can display this attribute by being upfront at the beginning of the presentation, stating facts like:

1. Outlining where the customer is currently with challenges, processes, tools, and needs

2. Depicting a semi-clairvoyant picture of where the cus-
    tomer wants to be
3. Avoiding aggressive and pushy tactics
4. Being frank and confident by telling them that the above
    facts remain regardless of who provides the solution

Like anything else, to move prospects, you need to be fully
prepared—even more so if presenting remotely—again, more
on virtual presentations at the end of this chapter. Start by
figuring out your presentation's narrative (storyline). Identify
the key points and purpose of your presentation. For example,
are you trying to:

1. Replace or unseat a current vendor?
2. Introduce a new technology?
3. Implement change?

Subsequently, you need to identify how you want the buyer to
react, what you want them to do. Your presentation's success
hinges on how clearly, concisely, and convincingly you answer
the following questions:

1. Why do you (the prospect) have to make a change?
2. Why now?
3. Why buy from me?

The above questions must be answered with confidence in
front of the prospect. One way to exhibit confidence is to start
the presentation with a question that will allow you to assess
the group's technical knowledge and indicate how deeply you
should go into technical details.

Most likely, you'll have people with a different business and/or technical backgrounds in the audience. Some will want a deep dive under the hood, some will want the 10,000-foot overview, and most will fall somewhere along the spectrum between the two.

Don't act desperate! Even if your career depends on the deal, the potential customer must not get any indication of that. Also, 1) never shy away from pricing and asking to move forward to the next steps, 2) don't spend too much time on yourself or your company, and more importantly, 3) never bad mouth competitors.

Set the Stage for Your Presentation

To set yourself up for the win, you need to ascertain some essential information such as who will be participating in person or virtually. With the help of your inside champion, learn the names, rank, and, if possible, attitudes of the participants and identify the decision-makers. Knowing participants' names allows you to look at their professional profiles and identify some of their needs in advance. With these arrows in your quiver, you are better equipped to relate to them personally and professionally during the presentation.

Remember, they may be doing their homework by researching you as well. This is another reason to make sure your online presence is clean and professional looking, displaying your expertise and trustworthiness. Earlier, you should have gathered valuable information about your potential customer's organization, current situation, and needs. However, at this stage, whether it is through research or via your relationships with an inside champion, you need to gather insight beyond the obvious, such as their current vendor or supplier or their economic and technical challenges or their purchasing process. It's also helpful to know some company-specific or industry lingo; using their vernacular, speaking their language can go a long way toward building a relationship.

Today, we often see the most well-versed and coached political candidates, corporate leaders, CEOs, and vendors—while carrying a great and motivating messages in their heads—fail to communicate effectively, usually because of the "tendency to go back to bad habits or their comfort zone during presentations," as described earlier. In our SaMA workshops, we work with salespeople, subject matter experts, and executives to overcome these challenges. Likewise, you have to seek this support from your sales team as well.

Below, we cover some of the best practices for effective presentation and go over some presentation dos and don'ts recommended by Kelly Robertson of Business Know-How, a business publishing group[3]

1. **Create a Connection Between Your Product/ Service and the Prospect:**

   Although you had already made these connections over the phone or on cocktail napkins with your potential customer during the previous phases, you have to remind them—and the other stakeholders in the room—of their current challenges. In other words, why are you there? Also, having a show and tell demo or a prototype they can feel and touch will make this bonding even stronger. As Michael Bosworth describes in *Solution Selling*, "The buyers must have a vision of the solution that they can see themselves participating in."[4] You can then tell your audience about product features and discuss the benefits. Tell your customer what they will gain by using your product. "Show me how this affects the bottom line. Is this going to grow our business?" as Corinne Nevinny (board member of Insulate Corp) advises.[2]

2. Get to the Point and Don't Over Deliver:

Today's businesspeople are far too busy to listen to long-winded presentations. Thus, you need to know who is in the room, understand their needs, and gauge their engagement. In other words, practice gauging the *receptivity* we talked about previously.

Unfortunately, a staggering number of mid-level sales-people—about 67 percent—come into top-level meetings and shoot themselves in the foot by:

1. Not stating what they want at the beginning.
2. Having too many PowerPoint slides.
3. Rigidly sticking to their script.

Know what your key points are and learn how to make and prove them quickly. On one occasion when I worked at Hewlett-Packard (HP), I accompanied one of our sales teams to a presentation to demonstrate a 24/7 high availability product—which at the time was the industry-leading solution for all mission-critical applications. After I did my POC (proof-of-concept) on how their enterprise application could successfully failover to another server in a cluster without any interruption or corruption to operations or data, the customer was ready to proceed to the next step, which was signing the purchase order. However, one of our salespeople continued by describing features the customer had already told us were unnecessary. At that point, the customer paused and started to pick apart those extra features—noting that he'd be paying heavily for features he would never use.

As a result of over-delivering by describing non-essential features, the customer closed their checkbook. The presentation stalled, and we could not salvage the deal. As the former executive chairman of NetApp—one of my previous employers— Dan Warmenhoven said, "The bottom line is, the statement you start with has to include all the key metrics: what's the investment, what's the return?"[2]

3. A More Effective Way of Presenting Features, Advantages, and Benefits:

Often during presentations, sellers use these words interchangeably. Although in the previous phases you were successful at helping your customer identify problems they needed to address, during the presentation you must avoid bombarding them with all the amazing, matchless features your product or service offers. As we discussed in the prospecting chapter, in solution selling, features should be used to prove a product or service can meet the buyer's vision. By participating in the buyer's vision, the seller becomes the person from whom the buyer will want to buy. According to *Solution Selling*, all features are advantages if 1) the "benefit" is in the mind of the buyer, not the seller, 2) the buyer has a vision in which the seller participated. And this pretty much explains the landmine my HP colleague stepped on. The real benefit statement should indicate that the seller's product or service can provide a solution in which both the seller and buyer participated.[4]

4. Content vs. Delivery Style:

The jury is still out on the relative importance of content versus delivery as to which is the key to a successful presentation. As an experiment, pick a couple of your favorite songs and/or movies. Now think about whether it was the words, the content, or the performance, the way they were delivered, that made them memorable? Did the content—lyrics/script—or the way the content was delivered—performance—make the difference? I'm sure for some people it can be one or the other. Of course, if you're presenting to executives, "Style is like icing on the cake. You can have a lousy style, but if you have good content, you'll still be successful," said Robert Drolet, a former defense industry executive.

Going back to the earlier *faux pas* during our HP POC presentation, George Gleeson, enterprise hardware sales manager at Oracle, reminds his sales staff to not make themselves the lead actors in the play. You are not!

"Go in there and quickly, concisely deliver the information, answer questions, survive it, and get out."[2]

The main takeaway is to never discount content or style! The two keys to any powerful presentation or performance—agreed upon invariably by all experts I spoke to or read—are content *and* delivery. That is, you must show passion and interest when presenting your offering to potential customers without drama or boredom. This is even more compelling when you're presenting remotely.

Whether in-person or remote (over virtual conferencing applications like Zoom, WebEx, or Skype), the listener must feel your energy, enthusiasm, and above all, your authenticity in the delivery of your message. To display this energy, presenters must possess effective verbal and non-verbal communication skills. The former includes the idea that verbal communication is more than words. That is, you have to use these five qualities to better capture and retain your audience's attention: 1) pace, 2) pitch, 3) tone, 4) volume, and 5) articulation.

Of course, with nonverbal delivery skills, the emphasis is on appearance and body language. To master these skills, you have to practice making eye contact, posture, poses (like crossing your arms or legs, etc.), movements, and facial expressions—which all should be totally congruent with your verbal communication.

Physical appearance is equally important. For example, wear neat, clean clothing that is appropriately formal for the situation, face and hair should be appropriately professional, etc. The idea is to eliminate distractions when you appear in front of your audience.

5. Take a Break From Slideshow and Start Whiteboarding

Although today's state of art electronic presentation tools from different vendors such as Freelance, PowerPoint, etc. have made the presentations easier, more colorful, and animated, the challenge of staying focused on the content and presenter have been magnified. Even the millennial sales force can attest how their schoolteachers projected confidence and control when they taught their classes just using the dry erase pens and whiteboards, let alone the veteran sellers who smelled and breathed chalk on the blackboards! After all, according to the king of animation, Walt Disney, "Of all of our inventions for mass communication, pictures still speak the most universally understood language." Many teachers and professors mastered that language by writing and depicting their thoughts using pen and board. Prior to the 1990s (before the birth of contemporary electronic presentation software), although today we consider those methods primitive, the focus was always on the speaker. Research by Kalina Chirstoff, Brain Research Center Professor at University of British Columbia, shows that everyone's mind wanders more than one-third of the time. According to the book *Whiteboard Selling* by Sommers and Jenkins, with whiteboarding, your customer will be less likely to be drifted elsewhere. In fact, the authors claim that, "when you are drawing, you are physically moving, because the human brain is programmed to pay attention to the movement. Whereas with PowerPoint which is more static, not much is moving...."

Thus, those speakers who did not have their back constantly facing their audience delivered more interactive and engaging sessions- contrary to most of the slideshow deliveries we are attending on a daily basis. According to Sommers and Jenkins, "When sales professionals lose the PowerPoint and use the pen, they are more confident, and they are much more likely to compel buyers to act..." Because of this, during the new hire workshop at my previous company NetApp, we provided the Sales & Marketing staff with a half-day session on the basic whiteboarding skills and communication. At the NetApp U., we knew the last time that the majority of the new hires had touched a pen and paper was when they signed their offer letters; yet, we had to prepare them to appear with the needed tools and knowledge to effectively communicate our solutions in front of the customers and executives. The intention was to make them mindful of the instances that they may not have access to a projector or maybe they have to show their solution on a cocktail napkin. In that workshop, we provided the basic skills and structure of whiteboarding, coupled with some hands-on activities on penmanship and drawing, as illustrated in Figure 6. The goal was to figure out how to transition from an unstructured and messy drawings (Figure 6-a) to more structured and intuitive whiteboarding (Figure 6-c) using some of the basic and frequently used drawing icons- examples shown on Figure 6-b. As the final project, we rehearsed how to take a potential customer—with only a pen and whiteboard—on a journey with our data storage and cloud technology solutions.

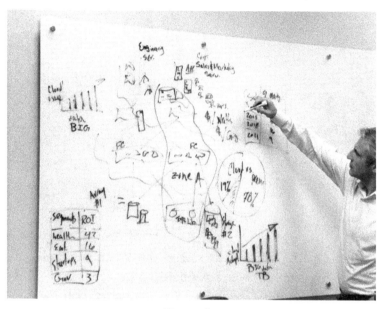

Figure 6-a.

Figure 6-b.

Figure 6-c.

One of the success stories the *Whiteboard Selling* alludes to is a report by Aberdeen Research titled "Train, Coach, Reinforce—Best Practices in Maximizing Sales Productivity" (October 2012). It revealed that conducting and leading an interactive whiteboarding as opposed to static slideshow leads to 50 percent higher lead conversion rate, 29 percent shorter sales rep ramp-up time, and 2.3 percent higher change in first year reps on quota.[8]

6. Presenting in a Second Language

For many on our sales staff, SMEs, and myself, English is their second language. Presenting in a language we learned later in life is challenging for many of us. Thus, in training and workshops, I encourage our English as a second language (ESL) participants to embrace their accents and use them to their advantage. *The Sales Engineering Handbook* provides this valuable guidance: "Since the audience will notice the accent, our advice is to deal with it upfront and, when introducing yourself, make some joke or comment about your manner of speech. The humor must be directed toward you and not the audience." [5]

The following story illustrates this advice. During my tenure with HP, we had a fairly large sales and training center in L'Isle-d'Abeau, France, an industrial town outside of Lyon. During my first visit to the center, I met John Kelly who was with our enterprise servers sales training group. John is Scottish. He told me he always starts his lectures with humor. "Folks, before I start, let me tell you that there is nothing wrong with the English you've all learned in school!" which implicitly points out his accent. He makes the audience aware of it to avoid possible distractions associated with his heavy Scottish accent. That self-deprecating but effective humor at the beginning of his classes is one of the greatest lessons I learned from a colleague, and I have tried to duplicate it in my own classes ever since.

Here are some tips for presenting effectively in a language other than your native tongue:

- **Enrich Your Vocabulary:** I and others recommend speaking conversationally, with a relaxed tone and manner that will hold the listeners' attention; however, consider using rich words to better connect with listeners. Just remember, words have denotations and connotations. Denotation is the precise dictionary definition and connotation is the wide array of positive and negative associations most words carry. This means you may have to go beyond the dictionary to ensure you are using words appropriately. Also, keep in mind, not all forms of the same word mean the same thing, so conserve and conservative are not at all the same. Remember, your customers talk to many vendors and listen to industry jargon daily. You need to differentiate yourself from the pack by showing your prowess in the language in which you are presenting.

- **Be a Communication Chameleon:** Top sales producers, regardless of their native tongue, are *communication chameleons* who can connect with any customer. They can adapt to any situation, which I defined earlier as situational fluency.[6]
- **Improve Your Pronunciation**: Fluency in a foreign language means more than mastering vocabulary and grammar. Improper pronunciation and intonation can break down communication quickly.
- **Speak Slowly:** On the day of the presentation, you can help your audience adapt to your accent by speaking clearly and talking slowly.

Although the above tips may be elementary, my colleague John told me he constantly needs to be mindful of them and not falling back into his natural conversational style and diction, which although perfectly understandable to other Scotts, may be unintelligible to others. And based on feedback from his students, he is able to speak at a proper pace and annunciate key terms clearly.

7. Believe in Your Product/Service

A good sales presentation can influence customers to buy from you instead of the competition. The quality of your sales presentation differentiates you from the competition, which often determines whether a prospect buys from you. The salesperson needs to wholeheartedly believe in what their product and/or service can do for the customer. Your command in verbal and non-verbal communication, coupled with your situational fluency, demonstrates the trust and belief you have in your offerings. After all, if you can't get excited about your product, how can you expect your potential buyer to get excited about buying it?

You can also portray confidence in your product by letting the potential customer take a demo or prototype for a spin. Work out a deal with your management to let the customer feel and touch the product or service by taking it on a test drive, so they may be convinced your solution will address their problem.

8. No Generic Presentations, Ever

One of the most common mistakes salespeople make when presenting their products or services is using a generic presentation. Marketing and engineering teams usually create sales and technical slides, whitepapers, briefing notes, and demos. Too often, salespeople rely solely on these off the shelf collateral materials for a series of presentations. This is a mistake.

Remember, one size does *not* fit all; thus, we must take the time and resources to adapt this generic information to tailored presentations for each potential customer. Customization does not have to be an arduous task. For example, when our team works with our SMEs and sellers to modify their generic content, only changing 10 to 20 percent of the material to reflect the intended audience's logo and other specifics, their message is better received by the customer. With those minor changes, the salesforce is able to show their solution in the context of the audience's organization by calling out their needs, challenges, and offering company-specific solutions.

One well-known example of a corporate *faux pas* fairly recently was when Nike lost Stephen Curry—the most sought-after point guard in the National Basketball Association (NBA)—to Under Armor. As reported by ESPN, during a presentation by Nike, a slide featuring Kevin Durant (another equally important but more senior NBA player) was left in the presentation by accident. Curry ended up signing a $4 million deal with the lesser-known sporting attire company, Under Armor. Don't fall into to the habit of reusing "canned" presentations; the audience can smell and recognize it from distance.

9. Engage and Interact With Your Audience

One unspoken rule of public speaking is, "you're presenting at the pleasure of your audience—not the other way around." It is very frustrating when stakeholders and executives become distracted or disengaged during a presentation. We all face this at some point. Yet, you have to deal with it. Of course, it is easier said than done, but you must keep your audience engaged.

If you have lost your audience, a pause or reiterating the agenda usually helps bring everyone's attention back. If that doesn't work, the presenter needs to get the champion involved to reengage everyone.

It is also important to *read* and get a *sense* of the room before jumping to the conclusion that the audience is not paying attention. The people in the room may be taking notes or fact-checking your points.

Avoid stuffing *too* much information on a slide. This will not help you interact with your audience. Too much content is distracting to any audience and will only lead them to tune out. Fewer slides with less content provides opportunities to interact and engage with your audience.

10. And don't Even Think About it

Don't even think of going to a customer presentation and/or demonstration without coordinating and planning your presentation with the technical presenter and the account manager! If you're co-presenting, you have to approach it as a team sport like football, soccer, or basketball. Only one person at a time has the ball, and the rest—on and off the field—provide support. Each person—whether a salesperson or account manager—can add or take away value from the presentation. Lack of coordination will bring the latter, causing confusion and possible errors or omissions. This is pretty much what happened during the HP presentation I talked about earlier.

Coordination and planning is more than a fifteen-minute huddle in the customer's parking lot. It goes well beyond that. Well in advance, you must: 1) storyboard your presentation and demonstration based on insights provided by the inside champion, 2) come up with your game plan—who says and does what, 3) structure and practice your whiteboarding on how to make your message across using drawings and writing, and 4) do at least one dress rehearsal.

"So let it be written. So let it be done." This is an example of how Chuck Tosch, Senior Application Engineer and Rick Browarski, Director of Product Marketing both with Infineon's Automotive division prepare, script and rehearse their roles and talking points prior to appear in front of distribution partners or customers. Although the emphasis should still be on an authentic presentation, knowing *who* to say *what* and *when* to- similar to the conversation flow and dynamics of the anchors and experts seen on TV during the NFL Sunday shows- will keep and retain your audience's attention on your message.

Also, it is valuable to have your management team or peers observe your rehearsal so they can provide feedback before you are in front of the customer.

Virtual Presentation

As an educator for the past twenty years, I have made my living by developing and delivering virtual and online courses both at the industry and academic levels—well before the era of WebEx, Skype, Zoom, and other virtual platforms—and I have learned a thing or two about developing and delivering content using these platforms. In the COVID-19 era, people worked and learned from home; businesses had no choice but to embrace virtual meetings and presentations. With the spread of the remote delivery and our dependence on it during the lockdown crisis, it is paramount to be mindful that "Communication tactics that work well among colleagues in a conference room may not translate seamlessly into Brady-Bunch-style quadrants on a computer screen," as Joel Schawartzberg, author and communication expert, said. So, these are the facts and realities of interacting and engaging with our colleagues, customers, and partners—even after we defeat the coronavirus and get back to business-as-usual!

Figure 7.

Before enumerating the key challenges of virtual presentations—some depicted as a joke in Figure 7, it is worth mentioning two very intuitive, yet important, factors of this method of interaction, as businesses are finding a number of advantages over F2F meetings:

1. Time, cost, and resource savings—No need to impress the customer with fancy clothes, shoes, cars, and meeting rooms. And certainly, it is a less expensive way for everyone to come together.
2. Recording your interactions with partners and customers—The most attractive feature is the ability to record your conversations. These recordings are gems that can be used for self-development, review, realignment, coaching, and sharing the conversations with sales teams. *But you have to ask permission from the presenter(s) (or disclose it with the audience) prior to recording*!

The single most challenging part of virtual presentations is keeping the audience engaged and interested. During your presentation—whether with the camera on or off—you're constantly swimming against the current—research shows 92 percent of your audience is doing other activities while you're speaking. If you must deliver virtually, please consider the following:

1. First things first. Now that you don't have to invest in fancy shoes and pants for your presentations, you must invest in technology. Invest in a robust and proven virtual platform and infrastructure that will facilitate a happy virtual experience for your clients, so they are more likely to want to come for more.

2. To reduce the number of distractions, you and your team must invest in bandwidth, a high definition camera, and a high-quality microphone. Otherwise, your delivery will be choppy, sketchy which may force people to leave the (virtual) room. Also, the background and lighting should be appropriately neutral to avoid causing additional distractions. For example, messy rooms, open closets, bathrooms in the view, and dark or extremely bright rooms will shift attention from your content to those distractions.

3. Preparation is the key to a successful virtual presentation. As a trainer, coach, and host, I've delivered content virtually every week for decades, and I know the ins and outs of many of these platforms; however, I can't describe the nervousness I experience before each call. Something almost always goes wrong, and often it's the things you least expect. In addition to dress rehearsals, you (and your team if presenting jointly) must log in twenty minutes prior to the call to check the connectivity, registrations, audio, video, slide sharing, and load your poll questions if you have them. Remember, if co-presenting, refrain from coordinating and/or going over the game plan during this time, as people are making their way into the virtual room and may hear your conversation. They appreciate presenters taking the time before the call to go over the technical details. You may come across as unprepared if you are heard and/or seen reviewing plans or reminding each other of your role in the presentation.

4. Now, on to the content. The final presentation is very different from the earlier exploratory presentations; thus, the only focus should be on your expertise

and the solution that will help the buyers solve their problem.

5. Do not start with the brag slides that talk about you, your company's history, and other customers whom you helped in the past. But certainly, toward the end, use them to cement your capabilities and expertise.

6. Your first slide should articulate their current situation or problem and how your recommended solution is going to address it.

7. Always follow the KISS principle! That is, "keep it simple, stupid!" When crafting your pitch and slides, you just need to create the desire (or an *aha* moment or a cliff hanger) within your audience's minds so they seek more information later.

8. Too many slides in your virtual presentation will hurt your chances of success. Keep the focus on you as a speaker by limiting slides and slide content. And watch your audience so you can pull them back into your talk if you see them drifting away.

In essence, virtual delivery starts with going over the ground rules with your audience. This is an opportunity you need to seize to show your command and control of the remote session. For example, you respectfully request that the audience put their phones or microphones on mute so there is no background noise that would disrupt your talk. Believe me, in my twenty years of virtual delivery, my students and I have heard it all: barking dogs, crying babies, toilets flushing, even intimate talks or couples fighting in the background. But fortunately, these days, participant lists on the major platforms clearly indicate who the noise culprits are so, as the host, you can mute them.

You also need to instruct the audience on how you want them to interact with you while you're talking, for example, via chat, raising their hand, or simply unmuting themselves, so you can field their comments or questions. From what we have seen, as more and more of these virtual sessions are conducted, people have acquired a great deal of acumen and ethics associated with how to behave during these remote sessions—both as speakers and audience.

According to Joel Schwartzberg, in his article "How to Elevate Your Presence in a Virtual Meeting," published in the April 2020 *Harvard Business Review*, "Elevating your presence in a virtual meeting requires not only engaging in video conference-friendly tactics but also disabusing yourself of potentially detrimental misconceptions about the medium."

Nevertheless, both the HBR article and my personal experience provide the following recommendations for delivering a more engaging and interactive virtual presentation:[7]

1. **Show your face:** Obviously, people relate to you better when they can see you, so invest in a high-quality USB camera with at least 720p resolution for your presentation.

2. **Focus on your camera, not your viewers:** Although keeping eye contacts with the audience is essential during meetings held under the same roof, in a video conference, eye contact means looking into the video camera, not at their smiling faces.

3. **Start with an ice-breaker:** Almost all meetings should start with an ice-breaker before getting into the topic. One good ice-breaker in a virtual meeting is

to start with a poll or a simple question. For example, "Who in the audience has heard of or used X product?" or "What are your top three challenges today?" These polls/questions must be *soft-ball questions,* not technical.

4. **Don't hide behind your slides:** When you are showing slides, the audience will see you in the *thumbnail* view, which is fine, since the focus should be on the slides you are sharing. However, for better interaction, engagement, and rapport with your audience, take a break from showing slides and appear in the *active speaker* display, which is a larger view of the person currently speaking. In this mode, you can ask directed questions and have a better view of the audience.

5. **Maintain a strong voice:** Even though you're using a microphone and thus may be tempted to speak at a conversational volume, maintain a strong, clear voice as if you're in a large conference room. Using a loud voice will keep you from mumbling and/or speaking too quickly.

6. **Frame yourself wisely:** In a video conference, your head and the top of your shoulders should dominate the screen. Although a cluttered background is distracting and unprofessional, some real or virtual backgrounds can also serve as great ice-breakers. For example, one of my former colleagues from NetApp, Patrick Reardon, decorates the background of his home office with golf clubs and nicely framed industry certifications and awards. Although simple and humble, "There is always a comment, question, or praise from the audience about these items at the start of each meeting," he claims. As a remote presenter, these

comments and questions put you at ease before the call because you instantly make the connections with some of your audience without saying a word.

7. **Be present and mindful:** Contrary to a conversational meeting, in a video conference where you're muted, it's easy to forget you're still being watched. You may be tempted to multi-task, checking email or surfing the web, which is perilous because you don't want to be caught unprepared if you are suddenly asked a question.

8. **Use the chat window as your partner**: Consider the chat window as more than a discussion platform, but also a presentation appendage. Chat is a great way to ask people to voice their comments and questions without interrupting the presentation. It elevates your presence and demonstrates that you're fully present.

Other Landmines:

1. Going Overboard With the Demo

Whether the demonstration is done in a room with the buyer or remotely, you must stick to showing them only the features that mattered most to them. Your product may have lots of great features and benefits but control yourself—don't go overboard demonstrating every cool and amazing feature.

Particularly, with virtual demonstrations, internet bandwidth, speed, and image quality are usually against you. Thus, do not rush through, clicking menu items or quickly jumping from webpage to webpage. Using a laser pointer or other annotation tool ensures you're navigating the content on screen sedately, while engaging and interacting with the audience to see if they are still with you.

2. Food Fight

Another landmine to be aware of is the executives' food fight. You, as the presenter—who is without any power or authority over the audience—should not get involved or chose sides in arguments between the executives in the room. The reason is simple. You are not going to win. Your role is to listen, attempt to refocus the group, and do your best to lead the conversation to your advantage. If all else fails, go to plan B and get your champion involved.

3. Weak Closing

Referring back to the attention chart shown earlier, just as you tried to capture attention with brief *problem, solution, payoff* statements at the beginning of your presentation, you want to close on a high note as well. Thus, as part of a strong finish, you want to conclude your talk by:

1. Solidifying your main points by repeating your key message(s) in your summary slide.
2. Outlining your expectations of the audience by presenting a *call-to-action* slide.

Your presentation is considered effective when all your points are clearly presented and reinforced by repeating the key points and requesting some easy to do tasks (such as downloading and playing with a demo or discuss the benefits of the product with customers, etc.) for attendees as action items. Most likely, they won't do those tasks; however, it certainly shows how serious and committed you are to their understanding the information you just presented. And as always, make yourself and the rest of your sales and technical team available to provide more information and expertise as needed.

The Last Word

We have all probably experienced the great feeling of thinking we aced a job interview based on impromptu responses from the hiring team, only to get the proverbial *thanks but no thanks* email. Naturally, we all feel great, empowered, and hopeful after a good sales presentation. Particularly when, just like a good job interview, we feel we showed ourselves and our offerings in the best light, answered all the buyer's challenging questions perfectly, and received approving nods from participants during and after the presentation.

Well, not so fast! During the presentation we may have aced explaining the features, benefits, advantages, quality, sales, price, cost of ownership, ROI, and then some but this is only 10 percent of the iceberg. The 90 percent you could not see is the CIO, CTO, and other decision-makers who can't help thinking about their current system, logistics, and vendor commitments before they can switch to your wonderful solution.

Summary

Making it this far is a major accomplishment for you. At this pivotal phase, we covered lots of ground, for example:

- Nothing is more compelling and essential than verbally demonstrating your understanding of the buyer's challenges and needs.
- A strong opening is key to a successful presentation—clearly state the *Problem, Solution,* and *Payoff* early.
- Be aware of landmines sellers frequently step on when they fall back into their comfort zone:
  1. Talking too much about one's self
  2. Showing to many slides
  3. Focusing on unnecessary features
  4. Failing to state the problem, solution, and payoff from the start of the presentation
- Both content and delivery are essential factors for a successful presentation.
- Practice your presentation to come across as authentic as you can instead of using a script.
- Your verbal and non-verbal communication skills are the keys to a more effective, moving presentation.
- Engage the audience quickly; successful presenters get to the point immediately; particularly, in the case of virtual presentations
- With whiteboarding, the drawing enhances what is being said; thus, visual storytelling is a better way to foster a two-way dialogue and built trust.
- The audience loves to be able to compare and contrast so they have a reference point.

- Never bad-mouth the competition; instead, differentiate yourself by articulating deep insights into the current market and competitive solutions.

Call2Action:

1. Enroll in a power speaking or presentation class.
2. If your job does not provide training, look for Toast Masters classes near you.
3. Toast Masters classes are a great way to practice your presentation skills and receive feedback from peers.
4. Watch numerous online videos on effective communication and presentations.
5. Strongly recommend reading *The communication Chameleon* by Claudia Ferryman, Rainmakers Books, 2011.
6. Strongly recommend you practice your penmanship and drawing skills and you read *Whiteboard Selling* by Corey Sommers and David Jenkins.

Bibliography

[1]: *Made to Stick: Why some ideas Survive and others Die*, Chip Heath and Dan Heath, Random House 2008.

[2]: *Speaking Up*, Fredrick Gilbert, Berrett-Koehler Publishing, 2013.

[3]: Kelley Robertson, Business Know-How https://www.businessknowhow.com/marketing/sales-presentation.htm.

[4]: *Solution Selling*, Michael T. Bosworth, McGraw Hill, 1995.

[5]: *Sales Engineering Handbook,* 3rd ed., John Care and Aron Bohlig, Artech House Publishing.

[6]: *The Communication Chameleon: How to Lead, Persuade and Influence in Any Conversation*, Claudia Ferryman, Rainmaker Publishing, 2011.

[7]: "*How to Elevate Your Presence in a Virtual Meeting*," Joel Schwartzberg, *Harvard Business Review*, April 2020.

[8]: https://www.richardson.com/en-gb/blog/best-practices-inmaximizing-sales_productivity/.

CHAPTER 5

Preparing for Objections!

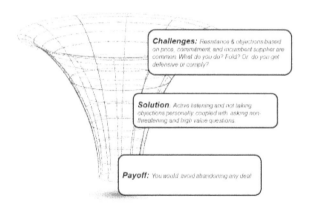

Challenges: Resistance & objections based on price, commitment, and incumbent supplier are common. What do you do? Fold? Or do you get defensive or comply?

Solution: Active listening and not taking objections personally coupled with asking non-threatening and high value questions.

Payoff: You would avoid abandoning any deal

Who's objecting now?

You, I, our friends, and our families can find objections when it comes to purchasing something—with more resistance when considering expensive items like cars, houses, or even, in my case, complaining about the high tuition price for my MBA program at a private business school. For most of us, as buyers, we resist by pointing to the price, budget constraints, lack of authority, timing, etc. After all, we use objections to keep sellers at bay, and at the same time, prove to ourselves we're in charge of the conversation.

Objections and Resistance are Fair Game

As you recall, one of the very first challenges in the *prospecting* stage was encountering resistance. The resistance came across as a bunch of excuses about time, price, budget, need, or whatever helped the leads or prospects get rid of the salesperson. As we've waded through the next phases of the sales process, those excuses by potential customers morphed into some legitimate concerns or conflicting feelings about the purchase. Thus, this module presents recommendations and solutions to add to your sales arsenal and use whenever you run into resistance.

Be cautious and ensure all future sales opportunities are founded on properly completed prospecting and qualification phases, done thoroughly. You will always encounter some objections down the road but if pricing, needed features, budgets, timing, authority, etc. have been addressed and pinned down in the earlier phases, they will not surface as problems later in the sales cycle.

Our cyber security sales vice president at OPSWAT said:

> Resistance may be due to product shortcomings during the discovery and proof of concept stages when the prospect is asking for deep discounts or delivery does not fit the prospect's timeline for general availability. In some cases, products do not come ready-made

and shrink-wrapped. Often, they require customization or professional services to deploy them. All these elements add to the complexity and can cause resistance.

By the way, do you remember a time when you left a presentation and you felt good about your performance, partly because you got the impression from the customer and your champion that you aced it? But, to your dismay, the deal was somehow stalled or completely derailed.

In the presentation chapter, we asserted that the benefits of your solution, its features, key distinction, price, and potential ROI constituted only 10 percent of the deal. The remaining 90 percent—using the metaphor of an iceberg with the majority of its mass hidden under the surface—is the deep discussions and hair-splitting arguments amongst the stakeholders, the CEO, and other C-suite executives involved. These concerns can stall any deal and many are beyond your control, such as financial, logistical, legal, etc. concerns. This is why sellers need to put heavy emphasis on learning about their customers' qualification criteria early on. Also, many internal discussions include concerns and objections raised by the business and technical decision-makers based on risk, implementation issues, and the adaptability of your solution. If your internal champion cannot intervene and/or influence key decision-makers, you may not be called back to explain or proceed to the next phase.

Preparing for Objections

As part of your due diligence and preparation for each phase, you must identify some of the most common objections that may be raised at any phase in the sales journey, such as price, features, competition, etc. In the prospecting module, we stressed the importance of *Fighting or Battle Guides* for all your products and services in preparation for when these concerns are raised. If you are prepared, you will be in a better position to effectively address any concerns.

One big challenge sellers encounter is addressing objections and concerns effectively when they arise and you are not in the room. For example, after your presentation, you may not be in the room when the stakeholders and key decision-makers discuss their questions and concerns. At this point, it may be too late to address their concerns as they raise them behind closed doors—you only learn about their concerns later. Remember, just because customers do not express objections, does not mean they don't have any.

You may hear or read different strategies from veteran sales professionals on how to handle some of these objections. For example, some recommend proactively bringing up the most common objections before the customer does. These experts believe that by raising these issues, buyers feel "this salesperson cares," which is one of the main attributes of the trusted advisor they want to see in you. Today, with the abundance of resources and data, the majority of the buyers are armed with competitive and technical information even before they interact with you; thus, they expect you to be upfront and address these issues before they do. Moreover, by being proactive the experts believe that the seller is in control of the conversation rather than being cornered or surprised when concerns are raised by the buyer abruptly.

Yet, other sales professionals believe that sellers should not volunteer information that could damage the deal. They do not see how disclosing weaknesses helps close deals or better address concerns. You can certainly argue both ways. However, I strongly suggest you work with your sales mentors, peers, and leaders to determine what has worked for them and what has not. These go back to the sales strategies and guidelines your organization adheres to, and as I suggested in the prospecting module, you should align your strategy with them.

First Things First: Listen!

And the second and third things on the list are don't get defensive or confrontational when encountering objections. They are not personal; that is, you have to realize that these are just questions and concerns from buyers to protect themselves and their organization against risks and potential hardship. Some may be valid, and some may well be off base; nevertheless, the buyer is entitled to raise concerns.

One more thing! Do not respond with the overused "thanks for your question" or "this is such a great question" or "we have been asked this question many times before" or any similar *evaluating* response. The potential customer can smell these scripted and artificial responses from miles away and it may be a turnoff. Instead, without making any assumptions, try to avoid sounding like you're trying to sell something. As I have recommended throughout the sales cycle, keep your response conversational so the potential customer does not feel they are being sold to.

Here are the four actions you *must* take when managing questions and objections before you address, overcome, or even ignore them:

1. Let Them Speak:

According to the *Sales Engineering Handbook* by John Care, 85 percent of objections and questions are brought up simply because the customer wants more information—not because they object to your proposed solution. Invariably, the most effective way to handle objections is to engage the buyer with some open questions in a two-way conversation. This will help you extract more valuable information to better understand their position. Subsequently, these additional and answers will help you remove obstacles.[1]

2. Make Sure You Listen Actively to Understand Their Concerns:

Don't cut the customer off! Instead, wait until they're finished and then repeat their concerns in your own words so they can gauge how well you understood—this helps eliminate misunderstandings that can torpedo any deal. The common mistake is trying to listen but being too anxious, too eager for our turn to talk, so we can defend our position and refute any criticism.

Instead, be patient. Wait, listen, and try to understand. Seeing things from the prospect's perspective and articulating their perspective builds trust and lets them know you can see things their way. It is also human nature to trust people who seem to understand and feel our concerns.

Here are some key techniques for building trust when by actively listening; you can be sure that your audience will understand from these behaviors that you are listening to their concerns:

- Paraphrase
- Clarify
- Ask questions
- Summarize
- Verbalize
- Weigh
- Read between the lines
- Carry the discussion forward

3. Respond Respectfully by Acknowledging Their Objections:

In the *Questions That Sell,* Paul Cherry states,

> Often, instead of listening to a customer's complaints and the specifics of their situation, sellers keep reiterating their positions, which makes them look arrogant and the customer ends up feeling that their input has no value. Once you internalize their concerns, you need to reassure them that the problem can be overcome.[2]

4. Satisfy and Put Objections to Rest:

Be sure to satisfy the prospect's objections and concerns so that they can be put to rest. It's important to pin down their main concerns to successfully address them. Don't let them grow into two or three more issues. You don't want to keep hearing "your pricing is too high," or "the value isn't clear" for their business, or "the service is too complicated" from them. If they are still asking, it's time to ask more probing questions as to why they are not satisfied with your responses. Once the objections and concerns are addressed, make sure you get confirmation and buy-in so you can put these issues to rest and move on.[3]

So, What Should I Do—Concede, Overcome, or Defer the Objections?

As stated before, the most predominant objections are price, budget, authority, and lack of features. Regardless of any given reasons, objections reveal we did not thoroughly perform the tasks in the qualification round. Also, do you remember the excerpts from *Solution Selling* we looked at in earlier chapters? We quoted: "The seller's tool for dealing with risks and objectives is the benefit statement, such as warranty, or the quality of the service, or more importantly, the saving on post-sale technical support and maintenance."[4] Most certainly, if your solution is lacking in any of these key areas, it reminds the buyer of their current pain and challenges and will prompt them to object about the above items. Below, we will look at two case studies in which the deal hit a road bump because of pricing and lack of features:

A. Objections Around Pricing:

Among typical objections, budget and pricing are the direst. If budget and/or pricing are blocking the deal, the seller has not successfully demonstrated their solution's value throughout the sales process, thus justifying the price of the product or service. In fact, according to a survey by Sales Insights Lab, more than half (55 percent) of respondents said that budget was either the first or second most common reason that strong sales opportunities fall apart.[4]

According to Stefan Michel, marketing consultant and dean at the International Business School in Lausanne, Switzerland, "While sellers compete on superior customer value, they lose business on price or sell too low." Thus, he recommends moving from cost-based pricing to value-based pricing. Of course, there are various pricing strategies and covering them all is beyond the scope of this book; however, suffice to say that *cost-based pricing* is *based* on the *cost* of production, manufacturing, and distribution. In this case, the *price* of a good is determined by adding a fixed percentage to the manufacturing *costs* to the selling *price* to make a profit. Although this pricing strategy is the simplest, it is flawed, as it ignores consumer demand and competitor pricing. It worth mentioning that this strategy is used by far too many executives and entrepreneurs.

The alternative, as Michel believes, is value-based pricing, as it is relevant for any organization regardless of size or industry. This method of pricing is determined by how much value your product or service adds for your buyer. For example, the perceived value of your product/service based on the prospect's happiness, ROI, ease of testing, ease of use, and other benefits.

Value-bases pricing not only helps determine what price your buyer is willing to pay, it also pushes your business to provide higher quality solutions and products.

Regardless of which pricing strategy you use, your potential buyer will still object. Although these pricing objections are common, they can be easily overcome. One of the techniques is a framework based on BayGroup International's methodology explained in *The Challenger Sale*. This four-step roadmap consists of:

1) Acknowledge and defer
2) Deepen and broaden
3) Explore and compare
4) Concede according to plan

For example, when the prospect voices price concerns and discount requests, the seller must acknowledge by saying, "I understand that we may be more expensive than other vendors, and…." Also, you want to supplement your acknowledgment with a permission-seeking request to defer the pricing discussion until after further exploration of your offerings by saying something like: "So, to make sure that I'm correctly addressing your concerns and making this deal as valuable as you need it to be…." This demonstrates that you were actively listening to their concerns. Also, by asking their consent to move forward, you show that you're listening to their concerns and not rushing justify the price tag on your service or product.[5]

If the salesperson does not secure the buyer's permission to proceed, further talk of value and benefits will fall on deaf ears—as the buyer is not going to listen to anything else the seller has to say.

But let's assume the buyer consents to hear more. This is when you want to deepen and broaden the prospect's understanding or your offerings and value they bring to the table. Experts believe that by bringing up the benefits and the tangible differences between your solution and your competitors, price concerns may become much less of an issue. All in all, by elaborating on the aspects of your solution that matter most to the customer, you help them visualize how they will benefit monetary, how easy the solution will be to use, and the superior quality. And without disrespecting incumbent vendors or rivals show how your solution is above the competition.

For example, this is how the medical device company in Toronto we talked about earlier overcame the money issue:

> For the clinical field, and especially in infectious disease, you would have an objection if the cost of your test is not reimbursed if no CPT (Current Procedural Terminology) code exists, or if it is not somehow covered by universal codes like DRG (Diagnosis-Related Group). Going into the specifics of these is a minefield but understanding how your lab gets reimbursed for their services will go a long way

to winning the money argument. Another tool we have used effectively is to build health, economic, or outcome models that clearly show how introducing a new test will save the hospital or organization money somewhere else.

B. The Proverbial High Price Objection:

This is one of the most common objections. In the earlier phases, the price objections usually have budgetary and affordability roots; however, buyers who complain about it at this stage may do so because of these two usual reasons: 1) slowing down the sales process, and 2) asking for a price reduction in the past has worked for them. On the latter, the most damaging action on the seller's part is to apologize and acknowledge the high price tag. Of course, with the understanding that the above acknowledgment is different from the "acknowledge and defer" step in the previous section, which was only to acknowledge their feelings and concerns. However, this price apology demonstrates the next two problems: 1) you are not fully prepared and lack the confidence to defend your price, 2) you don't believe in your offering or how it will address the buyer's needs.

According to Mark Hunter in *High Profit Selling*:

> It may surprise you, but when selling situations are consumed with discussion about price, it usually means that the salesperson is dealing with the wrong type of customer. You want customers who are focused less on price and

more on how your product or service meets their needs and delivers desired benefits.[6]

Confidence and belief in your products and/or services only come with copious preparation—you have to know your products inside out—and extensive market research. However, to withstand the *price-is-too-high* objection, you must stand firm. Otherwise, you give the buyer license for future haggling and discount requests. Particularly, if you are offering an innovative product as part of its *blue ocean* strategy; *blue ocean* refers to a market for a product where there is no competition or very little competition. This strategy revolves around searching for a business in which very few firms operate and where there is no pricing pressure.

Instead of affirming the buyer's claim, use situational fluency skills to confirm and defend the price, which was determined after extensive market research. Reference other buyers who were willing to pay the "ridiculously" high price. By doing so, you shift or deflect the price conversation to the value proposition conversation. Of course, you can offer to revisit pricing concerns later when looking at features and benefits during the course of the negotiation phase.

Finally, selling is challenging enough without annoying the prospect by prolonging the process. Despite all the efforts you pour into a deal throughout the phases, the customer may still not be convinced. They may not yet see the need or the value in your solution. The ROI may not be clear enough or may not fall in love with what you're offering. In such cases, you may find it more prudent to leave the customer alone and abandon the deal or yield to some of their conditions. In the former, you thank the prospect for their time and hope your paths cross again soon. Or you can make some concessions with your manager's approval.

Here is a customer story from our OPSWAT cybersecurity company's vice president where they had to yield to the customer's pricing objection:

We established close a partnership with a large vendor and they introduced a prospect that was using a solution offered by our partner. They were motivated by the promise of winning over a large public company and concurrently displacing a competitor. In the course of engaging the prospect, our sales team discovered the following: 1) our competitor was generating $900,000 per year with this account, 2) we could only offer them a 20 percent discount, and 3) the incumbent vendor offered to half the price. Eventually, the prospect's CIO told us that if we do not offer the solution at 10 percent of the original price, they would walk away. We ended up closing the deal at around $90,000. In the end, the prospect succeeded because we felt that having a major logo in our portfolio was more critical than an attractive profit margin.

C: Objections Around Features, Functionality, and Competition:

Objections about features and functionality, or lack thereof, are another conspicuous set of objections that are often heard from potential buyers. This is usually the result of landmine competitors put in place knowing your solution lacks certain features. Also, this may be of a way for the buyer to say, "Can you do X, Y, and Z like your competition does?" or "We want these features instead of the ones you're pitching." The good news with this type of objection is that the prospect is showing some interests in buying your product or service.

"To overcome these objections, first, we start with not bad-mouthing the competition," according to the SE senior manager at Oracle talking about how his team handles such cases. He continues:

> You should acknowledge them [their concerns] but then go deeper into their reasoning and see why your customer needs these features. Customers throw a bunch of features at our team that obviously came out of our competitor's datasheet. We pointed out that the competitor may have been just trying to fill up the data sheet with these features without understanding their relevance to the use case at hand. Many of these features were not the main requirements of the customer but nice to have. This method of dealing with objections only works if your core features are much stronger than the competitor and you can save the client time and money in its main requirements.

To succeed in going head-to-head with the competitions and shutting down their features and attractive pricing you must have:

1. Help and insights from your inside champion to guide you in the right direction.
2. Thorough knowledge of your and the competitions' product features and functionality.
3. An adequate understanding of your game plan and the strategy stated in your sales and marketing *fighting* guide, which, as I described in Chapter 1, contains product positioning and competitive analysis.

The Last Word on Value Justification:

The objections and concerns did not just surface in this phase of the sales cycle and most certainly will come up again in the next phases of negotiations and closing the deal. Based on the teachings of Learn Vision, a leading global sales training provider, most objections can be resolved with selling skills—as long as the salesperson consequently concentrates on ensuring customer satisfaction. Successful salespeople always try first to use selling skills to understand the objections better. Therefore, it is important to understand the objection clearly. Explore the background and then use your selling skills to:

- Present appropriate proof when the customer is doubtful.
- Resolve misunderstandings by presenting the benefits.
- Compensate for an expressed disadvantage through other advantages.[7]

Remember, negotiation only occurs if the salesperson cannot resolve objections, which is the topic of the next chapter.

Summary

Objections and concerns did not surface in this phase of the sales cycle, and most certainly, salespeople will hit these bumps again in the next phases—negotiation and closing the deal:

1. The bumps may be due to mishandling the qualification and discovery phases when assessing the prospect's BANT criteria.
2. Buyers may use objections as a tool to keep salespeople in check while allowing salespeople to feel are in control.
3. Not all questions are objections; many are valid concerns resulting from the seller's failure to show value and ROI during the sales cycle.
4. When dealing with objections, remember the followings:
   - Listen carefully and actively, don't interrupt, and repeat their concerns back to them in your own words to show understanding.
   - Make sure you completely understand their objections without making any assumption.
   - Respond respectfully by acknowledging their objections and making sure you've satisfied all their objections before moving forward.
   - No matter what the customer's objection, you can always find some points of agreement that you can then use to keep the conversation going.

5. To overcome objections, always go back to the value your products/services provide in addressing the prospect's pain.

6. Have a plan in place for dealing and/or complying with objections—what are you willing to concede, what can be overcome, what can be deflected?

7. Budget and pricing are the most common reason stronger deals fall apart.

8. Using value-based pricing confirms that your buyer is interested in what you have to offer based on value.

9. To avoid unnecessary objections and the perception of offering *fluff*, only present features that meet the prospect's stated needs.

10. To be fully prepared to combat pricing, features, and competition objections you must:
    a. Know your product's features and functionality inside and out.
    b. Know the pain and challenges your customer facies even better than they do.
    c. Fully study your *fighting* guides.
    d. Know the competition thoroughly.
    e. Get the support and help of your inside champion.

Call2Action

Review your company's selling guide to see if the most common objections are addressed.

1. Work with veteran and/or top performers in your office to see how they handle these common objections.

2. Proactively update your inside champions on any new developments that may help them help you succeed with the buyers.
3. Consider sales and negotiation training by well-known industry providers such as Learn Vision. info@ LearnVision.net.

Bibliography

[1]: *Mastering Technical Sales:The Sales Engineering Handbook*, 3rd ed. John Care and Aron Bohlig. Artech House Publishing, 2014.

[2]: *Questions That Sell: The Powerful Process for Discovering What Your Customer Really Wants.* Paul Cherry. AMACOM Publishing, 2006.

[3]: *9 Common Sales Objections (+How to Overcome Them).* Itamar Gero, March 2019. https://learn.g2.com/sales-objections.

[4]: *Mastering Sales Objections.* Marc Wayshak of Sales Insights Lab. June 2019. https://www.marcwayshak.com/sales-objections-overcome/.

[5]: *The Challenger Sale.* Matthew Dixon and Brent Adamson. Penguin Books, 2011.

[6]: *High-Profit Selling:Win the Sale Without Compromising on Price.* Mark Hunter. American Management Association, 2012.

[7]: *Negotiation for Sales.* Dusseldorf, Germany: Learn Vision, 2015. www.LearnVision.net.

CHAPTER 6

Negotiation Phase

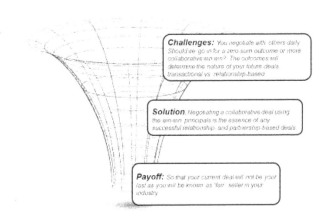

Challenges: You negotiate with others daily. Should we go in for a zero-sum outcome or more collaborative win-win? The outcomes will determine the nature of your future deals: transactional vs. relationship-based.

Solution: Negotiating a collaborative deal using the win-win principals is the essence of any successful relationship- and partnership-based deals.

Payoff: So that your current deal will not be your last as you will be known as "fair" seller in your industry.

We don't have to be in sales to take part in negotiations. In fact, all of us—from the womb to the tomb—both at the personal and professional level, constantly engage in various daily negotiations. We negotiate with ourselves, our parents, siblings, friends, roommates, teachers, spouses, kids, colleagues, managers, merchants, or anyone with a different interest or perspective. And needless to say, the goal in all our negotiations, unconsciously, is to win. We've systematically been taught that we should neither compromise nor quit until we get our way. With this zero-sum mentality, unfortunately, neither buyers nor sellers realize their current transaction may be their last. The word about our lack of collaboration or compromise and our thirst for winning at all costs gets around very quickly within our industry or community. Hence, if either party gets the feeling that they got the short end of the stick in a deal, they will likely name and shame the sales representative in the form of bad references or reviews, which may translate into loss of not only repeat business but also a drought of new prospects.

What This Chapter Is and It's Not About

The topic of negotiation and all its best practices is very lengthy and broad. Hence, covering all aspects of negotiation is beyond the scope of this book. As a salesperson, you were likely provided training and coaching on this subject. If not, you owe it to yourself to take a well-established course or seek peer mentoring in this field—without these basics, you won't be able to survive the unforgiving world of sales. It only took me three short months to bow out of my computer peripheral sales job I talked about at the beginning of this book. Back then, the company believed their sales force would pick up the needed skills via osmosis, by simply talking to customers over the phone! As a result of this misguided approach, and despite hiring more inside sales staff, sales plummeted despite the growing demand for products like theirs to make the PCs and workstations run faster and store more data with non-OEM accessories. And after only two years, they went out of business.

In this chapter, we will focus on the most common sales challenges, both in buying and selling, most face during the negotiation process.

Four Principles and A Model to Remember

Negotiation is how problems and conflicts are resolved. The goal is not just to make a deal; instead, the goal is to make a good deal that benefits both sides. Often, both buyers and sellers make common decision-making mistakes based on their egos or lack of flexibility. You may have seen the classic Thomas Kilmann model (TK model)—shown in Figure 8—in other sales and professional courses and literature. Given your sales and business acumen, I'll refrain from explaining the five boxes within the axis. But suffice to say that it is intuitive that based on your level of relationship and your outcome anticipation you and your buyer may leave something on the negotiating table. Another thing which is true is that throughout our personal and professional lives, we all experienced landing on all five of these boxes during any of our past negotiations or conflicts. Now, if we start to connect the dots and remember some of those past outcomes, we can agree that whenever we found ourselves in the collaborating box, we felt the most joy and satisfaction—joy and satisfaction none of the other boxes offered.

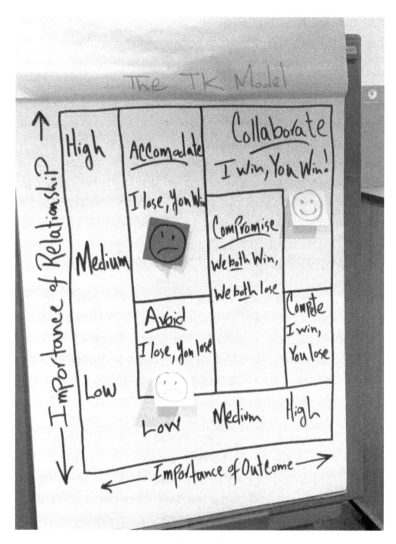

Figure 8

So, just like with presentations, there are three types of deals or term negotiations: 1) the one that you had prepared yourself for, 2) the one that you get, and 3) the one that you wished had all the terms and conditions you always wanted. The latter has to do with the degree of your rigidness and malleability. Thus, there is no perfect deal for any side—only the one that came close to your initial wants. In successful negotiations, both the salesperson and their organization should also profit; this is where both types of needs (organizational and individual) are satisfied. As with all the previous phases, it is all part of preparing before you meet face-to-face with the perspective buyer. So, here are the four key principals. There are many others, many of which you may already know or have practiced in previous negotiations:

1. Attacking the Problem Without Drama:

As you can see in the TK model in Figure 8, as the level of relationship increases, so do the emotions. As a result, the outcome of the negotiations will only satisfy either the seller or the buyer and not both. We also have to recognize this fact of human nature that our counterparts, whether friends, family, colleagues, or merchants, will put their interests above ours in any deal. And vice versa. We as a seller have the same propensity as our buyers to defend and guard our interests during negotiations. So, we should not take the objections and negations personally nor dismiss them as nonsense. On each side of the bargaining table, the people have certain intrinsic and extrinsic mandates, demands, and interests that must be addressed. For example, according to the experts in *Learn Vision*, customers are under pressure to purchase products and services at the best possible price for their organization. Often, the organization has guidelines and policies that require the customer to secure three or more quotes for a specific product or service. As a result, the customer often must negotiate with the sellers before closing the sale.[1] In other words, understand and respect your buyer's constraints when they reject what you feel is a sound offer.

2. Focus on Interests, Not Positions:

This is one of the main elements of principled negotiation described in the book *Getting to Yes* by three Harvard university professors, William Ury, Bruce Patton, and Roger Fisher. The best approach for this challenge is understanding the buyer's perspective before you start negotiating. The goal here is to understand their angle and intentions so you can better align their incentives with yours. Stephen Covey, in his successful book *The 7 Habits of Highly Effective People*, refers to this as building *emotional equity*. Other experts believe the better people know you, the faster they can trust you—maybe even trusting you before you walk into a room with them. Or in the case of a virtual negotiation, putting the face to the voice during an ice-breaker session.

Building a relationship and trust is all part of the preparation you need to do. In fact, in a study conducted by Adam Galinsky, a Columbia Business School professor and the author of *Friend and Foe*, discovered that when sellers take their prospect's perspective into account before negotiations, their success rate is **76** percent. In comparison, those who go into negotiations using the empathy approach were only 54 percent success-ful.[2] This shows that if both buyers and sellers focus on collaborating to satisfy certain areas of interests, like meeting quarterly quotas, acquiring more startup customers, cost-savings, ease of use with better ROI for their stakeholders, more precise instrumentation, etc., negotiations will be more productive, leading to a faster close.

Conversely, if both sides are steadfast in their own po-sitions, negotiations are doomed to fail. For example, if the seller wants to maintain their 63 percent margin on all sales no matter what the buyer's purchasing redline is or if the buyer merely fixated on a price without taking into the account the total value of the package offered, which includes items like maintenance, financ-ing, and warranty, then obviously, nothing good will come out of the negotiation.

3. **Considering Making Multiple Offers or Putting Together a Package:**

Speaking of package deals, making a single offer leaves little room for negotiating. As a result, you may not have room for further talks. Moreover, if the buyer re-jects or dislikes that single offer, what can the seller do next? In this case, instead the seller back paddles grasping for an alternative. It is advantageous for the seller to start with multiple offers. The key factor then becomes how these offers are framed; that is, ensure you stress what the other party would gain at the end of the negotiation.

According to Katie Shonk, the editor of Harvard Law School's Negotiation Briefings, "When you present multiple equivalent simultaneous offers (MESOs), you show other parties the issues you value the most. In turn, their reactions tell you about their priorities."

Here is an example that clearly explains the MESO:

> During the negotiation phase, a software company presented three equivalent software packages to its client at once, a $1 million package with payment due in thirty days, the same software for $1.5 million with payment due in 120 days, or an enhanced package for $1.35 million with a payment due in thirty days. Their potential buyer, who had expressed a lengthy budget approval cycle, responded well to this strategy, and the company's profits rose.[3]

Always Know Your *BATNA* When Entering Into a Negotiation

BATNA stands for your Best Alternative to a Negotiated Agreement which according to Guhan Subramanian the executive committee chair of Harvard Business School's Program on Negotiation, is among one of the many pieces of information negotiators seek when formulating deal-making and negotiation strategies. If your current negotiation reaches an impasse, what's your best outside option? That is, having a strong outside alternative enables you to walk away from a deal that doesn't meet your needs or that would compromise your vision or ethics.[4]

Of course, as we stated above, it is beyond the scope of this book to tackle every type of BANTA; however, suffice it to say that according to the basic negotiation theory, your BATNA should be the benchmark by which you compare the offer at the bargaining table with the best you could get if you walked away. If negotiations lead both the seller and the buyer to achieve their interests and objectives, then that's all upside. If not, there's no reason to agree.

Yet negotiators often neglect an equally important step: analyzing the other party's BANTA. Although finding out what alternatives the other party has can take some detective work, it can be well worth the effort. If you find that your counterpart has few options, then that knowledge can empower you.

Also know if both parties carry a high BANTA, the negotiation is less likely to succeed. Whereas, if one side carries a lower BANTA, than the other, chances of a fruitful negotiation are very high. Finally, here are few tips on your BATNA, according to Harvard University's program on negotiation:

I.   Two (or More) BATNAS Are Better than One.
II.   Don't reveal a weak BATNA.
III. Don't let them diminish your BATNA.
IV.   Research the other party's BATNA.

Avoiding Common Negotiating Traps

Understanding the Thomas Kilmann (TK) model and the four main principals from the earlier section is the easy part. They reveal an intuitive framework; however, implementing them during your next negotiation requires ample preparation and coordination with your sales team. By holding a negotiation strategy planning meeting with your sales and marketing teams, you will be more prepared to gather information and market intelligence. That is, whether you're selling a used car, professional services, or a company product, you want to maintain *information asymmetry*. That is, be fully prepared before you sit down to negotiate, you must know more than the prospect does about: 1) your solution (including all its features, strengths, and weaknesses), 2) your solution's position in the competitive landscape, 3) buyer's competition and current suppliers, and 4) pain and challenges your buyer is currently dealing with.

Here are some typical traps identified by the Harvard law school daily blog:

1. Overvaluing Your Possessions:

The endowment effect leads us to have an unrealistic assessment of just about anything we own, no matter how trivial. Thus, ensure as a seller you have done due diligence on the current and future market values of your products or services.

2. Focusing Too Much on Price:

In the previous chapter, we alluded to the pricing issue when it comes up as an objection. However, it is a fact of life that attractive pricing is the most important thing in the minds of both sellers and buyers during the course of negotiation. Again, according to Katie Shonk of Harvard Law School, "Self-interested focus on price will prevent us from viewing sales negotiations as collaborative." Thus, avoid mindless haggling; instead, negotiate multiple factors simultaneously. For example, entertain terms and conditions on delivery timing, payment schedules, and other sources of synergy that would enhance the agreement and your bottom line, such as your exceptional post-sales support.

3. Don't Let the Negotiation Ends at *No*:

Yes, during the objection phase we recommended that at a certain point you have *to* take no from the buyer gracefully. However, at this late stage—at the negotiation table—when the discussions are about the most favorable terms and conditions for each party, it is not prudent or advantageous for the seller to end with no. Even when getting past differences is unlikely and closing next to impossible, the seller must find a way to get a yes. If all else fails, do your best to get a clear explanation about their no stance, so if another opportunity manifests, you will know where disconnects were.

4. Making Unappealing Offers:

You need to have a vision of what your ideal outcome looks like after each round of negotiation. Also, you need to have some idea as to what the prospect's is. Sometimes, negotiators think they can establish dominance by making an extreme offer. However, this method backfires and has a chilling effect. When offers are so outrageous the other party loses all motivation to continue negotiating, the negotiations are doomed according to Professor Leigh Thompson of the Kellogg School of Management.[5]

Getting Ready for More and More Virtual Negotiations

As alluded to in the previous chapters, as part of lockdowns and working remote due to the COVID pandemic, sellers must embrace the fact that many of their deals will be negotiated virtually. Many people overlook these challenges and claim that virtual buying and selling are nothing new—citing the facts that we have been selling and buying online on Amazon, eBay, Craigslist, and other online platforms for decades. True! However, they are not recognizing that most of their buying and selling were transactional purchases and often did not require any negotiations. As the deals and price tags of your offerings go up, the potential customers want to negotiate terms and conditions in person. In Chapter 5, we made you aware of the best practices of virtual presentations for more effective delivery and demonstration to the buyers. You have to remember we are in the infancy of conducting many of our sales activities virtually or in hybrid, and the experts are completing their playbooks as more and more deals are negotiated in these new modalities. So, while the jury is out on what works well and what will not, the experts unequivocally agree that it is important for the buyer to see and hear the seller during the negotiation phase. According to Heiko Schickel, the Executive VP of Sales and Marketing Transformation at Infineon Technology in Munich, sellers must be mindful of certain challenges and trends when negotiating virtually. His team of functional leaders and procurement specialists recently negotiated a successful consulting contract using this modality, and these were some of his main observations:

1. The negotiation sessions—which might have taken hours or days in the past—will be much shorter when it's done remotely behind web cams.
2. In virtual negotiations, it is very hard to read the room and have hands on the pulse of participants' emotions.

He also sees the following major implications based on the above observations:

1. Shorter sessions force all participants to be more focused, precise, and crisp in their descriptions and statements but also opens up room for potential misunderstandings. In absence of more time and emotional context, negotiators run the risk of neither surfacing, nor clarifying them.
2. Equally, the sellers must address all the issues, provide answers to open questions, and get to the resolution faster almost instantaneously, which may not necessarily lead to the best result for both buyer and seller.
3. It is challenging for all parties involved to effectively sense the body language of the people in the (virtual) room; and it is becoming more challenging as the number of people increases on a video conference.

All in all, inevitably sellers must embrace this method of negotiation and try to mimic all the F2F activities virtually. And yes! It is going to be more challenging when your counterparts decide not turn on their cameras due to a bad hair day or saving on more bandwidths during the remote sessions.

Handling the Give and Take of Negotiations

Believe in your position and have confidence in your solution's value—without being arrogant. Hold your ground without underpricing yourself but be flexible on the outcome. You have to make adjustments as you go along. But still, your vision remains the same. Uncover the thing that matters most to the buyer and doesn't matter to you, and give it to them. You can then focus on your vision and little things will not derail the negotiation. Leave something on the table for them. All in all, roll with the punches—as long as it does not compromise your vision. For certain, you all have heard about which one is more important: winning a war or just a bunch of battles? Well, this is how Tamara Heath-Underbrink, the vice president of Sales & Distribution at Infineon Technology, put this proverbial maxim into perspective:

> You don't have to win each battle as long as you win the war. This will also allow the others to feel like they won from time to time but keep the strategic *big* goal in mind vs. making sure to win each discussion. Naturally, the human mind will be a little more open to allowing you to win (if you have the business case to justify).

Price Negotiation vs. Cost Justification

In the previous chapter, we defined two different pricing strategies, cost-based pricing and value-based pricing. The latter requires you to estimate the importance, worth, or usefulness of your solution to your buyer. Remember, *price* is a reflection of the confidence the customer has in you and your products.

The more confident you are as a seller, the more confident your customer will be. Glenn Magnuson, the vice president of sales at the Qvella Corporation, explains:

> In my experience, price negotiation is when you have a commoditized product or the customer perceives your product as commoditized. You sell on price and not added value. Price justification is when you "sell" your product. You look at all the benefits it can bring. For example, the reductions or value it brings in other areas, i.e., labor, control savings, calibration savings, length of stay savings, reduced turnaround time, etc. You get something (higher price) when you can justify other savings.

Don't Give Without Getting!

Understanding the buyer's price-value relationship is key. Asking about their sales process, critical needs, and timing are all essential factors to negotiate without giving discounts. For example, the same Qvella VP of sales, adds:

> If a customer asks for a price concession, work to get something in return. More terms on the contract, block out the competition for the future; that is, if I get you this price, let's agree that you are not going to ask me for another price concession when a competitor knocks on your door.

In the end, if the salesperson considers the four conditions of buying signal, customer needs, submit offer, and objections, then the chances of both sides winning increase. You should always consider these four conditions before you negotiate.[1]

"Whoever makes the first offer loses!" Myth or Truth?

Only a myth, Deepak Malhotra of Harvard University and the author of *Negotiating the Impossible* strongly disagrees with this notion. He believes that the seller will have more control of the conversation if they put the first offer on the table. By doing so, Malhotra argues the seller lays out the scope and framework of the deal, leaving the buyer to react.[6] Similarly, a study by Professor Leigh Thompson of the Kellogg School of Management showed a powerful positive effect when making the first offer. "The negotiator who puts the first offer on the table has an advantage, other factors remaining constant. That means that if you and I have done equal preparation and have similar leverage points, you will have an advantage if you make the first offer."[5] For example, during the pricing, if the seller puts out a $100 initial offer on the table, the final negotiated price would be closer to this number versus letting the buyer suggest an initial $50 price. Of course, many experts believe that for majority of the B2B and B2C transactions, it is the sellers who will make the initial bid or quote. For them, the more important concern should be the construct of the offer and how they justify it.

Therefore, from classrooms to negotiation tables, Qvella's VP of sales explains: "When you have presented an offer and if there is a silence, *don't talk*! If you start talking, you will lose control and then you are answering questions from the customer instead of asking them and being in control. Wait for the customer to re-spond. Once they respond, try to pin them down." For example, if they state the price is too high, then respond with more ques-tions to gain control and understanding. Keep asking questions that move you toward a point where you can strike a deal.

Women in Negotiations

This is a dangerous subject for a man to write about. I under-stand; but the topic is very near and dear for me. Because I am surrounded by two wonderful daughters, one of whom just started her sales career with a Fortune 10 company, an amazing wife with an extensive technical sales and marketing background, two professional grandmothers, and two aunts with distin-guished careers in engineering, college education, pharmacy, and sales and marketing, respectively. Of course, the family tree does not end here! I have half-a-dozen young and smart nieces that I am envisioning bright professional careers for. Although it will be years before some of them sit at a negotiation table, either face to face or across a screen, I'm extremely concerned about the disadvantages they may face in those situations.

Beyond today's pay and promotion disparities between male and female professionals doing the same job, there are addi-tional challenges and an uneven playing field in the workforce in general. According to research conducted by Australian profes-sors Mara Olealns, Ruchi Sinha, and Carol Kulik, because of the current challenges, women and men experience negotiations differently. They also show just how much gender stereotypes underpin women's experiences, both in how they perceive ne-gotiations and how they are perceived as negotiators.[7]

Other barriers women negotiators face include the likelihood of being lied to during negotiations. At UC Berkeley (where I spent years as an adjunct faculty teaching IT courses), researchers Laura J. Kray and Alex B. Van Zant, along with Jessica A. Kennedy of the University of Vanderbilt found in their recent study that women were lied to more often because participants viewed them as less competent than men and thus less likely to question their lies. Both men and women were more likely to give male negotiators preferential treatment by disclosing their hidden interests.[8]

Women Have Lower Expectations:

According to Professor Maggie A. Neale, a co-director of Stanford University executive program for women leaders, when it comes to negotiating salaries, women are not prepared. According to her, "Often you'll see that even when women say, 'I should negotiate,' they don't do a good job preparing by knowing how much more they want and why. They don't know how to tell their counterparts persuasively why they should get what they want." Neale identifies "lower expectations" as a key, explaining: "The problem with having systematically lower expectations is that you get systematically lower outcomes because expectations drive behavior. So, they get less not because they are women, but because their expectations are lower."[9]

Negotiation Tips for Woman

Katie Shonk from Harvard's program on negotiation recommends these three negotiation tips that focus on negotiating skills and tactics that women can use to achieve better results at the bargaining table:

Negotiation Tip #1
Be non-threatening. Past advice from experts such as Facebook COO Sheryl Sandberg has encouraged women to combine an assertive message with smiles, friendly gestures, and other non-threatening and traditionally feminine behavior.

Negotiation Tip #2
Be a team player. Women have also been encouraged to increase the odds of getting what they want by pointing out how their requests would benefit the organization rather than just themselves. This approach can work because it conforms to the gender stereotype that women are particularly concerned about others.

Negotiation Tip #3
Defensive measures. Women, in particular, can guard against being taken advantage of in negotiations by engaging in thorough preparation and testing their counterparts' claims.

The same sales and distribution executive at Infineon Technology shared her recent negotiation experience with respect to above researches and tips like this:

> The team player is a big one; in my experience this is a gap for men sometimes vs. woman. I have found especially for internal negotiations, getting alliances *before* the group negotiations, getting the buy-in of key

stakeholders will help minimize the "lies" or "perception generalizations" that can derail others involved to not look at the data. This takes time but can truly help let the data dictate vs. opinion statements.

Wrapping Up Negotiations

Finally, for both parties to determine if a counter-offer is acceptable, all possible alternatives must be clearly communicated. For that, the following steps are helpful: 1) Repeat alternatives and their benefits, 2) confirm overall solution accepted on both sides, and 3) discuss the next steps for closing the deal.[1] The latter is the subject of the last chapter of this book.

Summary

1. The goal of negotiation is to confirm the details of the sale.
2. Seller will have to withstand some squeezing but it is all part of selling.
3. Many salespeople lock themselves into a position either because of their egos or over confidence in their offering.
4. When to walk away from a negotiation is determined by your BANTA. This means a negotiator should know their BATNA or best alternative they will accept.
5. The TK Model and the four principals of negotiation must be looked at through the lens of what you want to accomplish during this phase.

6. Having a clear and practical BANTA is key in successful negotiation.
7. It is a good practice to compromise on something—as opposed to zero-sum negotiations that stall and fall apart much of the time.
8. Avoid common sales traps like an unrealistic view or assessment of your product or services.
9. Avoid talking too much; when you do talk, ask the right questions. The "right questions" vary throughout the sales process.
10. Practice active listening—you will gain more info and the prospect will trust you more. The more you let the customer talk, the more they feel connected to you; thus, you will gain valuable insights that will help you during the deal.
11. With increased confidence, women will be more likely to assert their needs. Also, confidence may also reduce anxiety about negotiating, which women experience to a greater degree than men.

Call2Action

1. Roleplay your next negotiation with managers and/ or peers. Their feedback can help a great deal in your negotiations.

2. Study the TK Model and listen to various podcasts and watch videos from Stephen R. Covey, the author of *The 7 Habits of Highly Successful People*.

3. Strategize and coordinate your next negotiation formally with the account manager and subject matter experts.

4. Consider getting sales and negotiation training by a leading provider such as Learn Vision. *info@LearnVision. net.*

Bibliography

[1]: *Negotiation for Sales*, Learn Vision Co. Dusseldorf, Germany 2015 WWW.LearnVision.net.

[2]: *Friend and Foe:When to Cooperate,When to Compete, and How to Succeed at Both*, Adam Galinsky and Maurice Schweitzer, Crown Publishing Group, 2015.

[3]: *Framing in Negotiation, Offer Manageable Options to Your Counterpart*, Katie Shonk, Harvard Law School, June 2020.

[4]: *"What is BATNA? How to Find Your Best Alternative to a Negotiated Agreement,"* Guhan Subramanian, Harvard Program on Negotiation, March 2020.

[5]: *The Truth about negotiations*, 2nd edition, FT Press publishing, June 2013.

[6]: *"Control the Negotiation Before It Begins,"* Deepak Malhotra, *Harvard Business Review*, December 2015.

[7]: *"Three of the Most Common Challenges Women Face In Negotiations,"* Mara Olealns, Ruchi Sinha and Carol Kulik, *HBR*, September 2019.

[8]: *"Not Competent Enough to Know the Difference? Gender Stereotypes about Women's Ease of Being Misled Predict Negotiator Deception,"* by Laura J. Kray and Alex B. Van Zant, and Jessica A. Kennedy, Vanderbilt University, Owen Graduate School of Management, Dec 2014.

[9] *"Why Women Must Ask (The Right Way): Negotiation Advice from Stanford's Margaret A. Neale,"* Vicki Slavina, Forbes.com, June 2013.

CHAPTER 7

Deal Closure

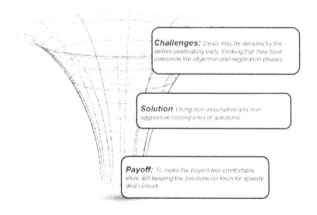

Challenges: Deals may be derailed by the sellers celebrating early, thinking that they have overcome the objection and negotiation phases.

Solution: Using non-assumptive and non-aggressive closing lines of questions.

Payoff: To make the buyers feel comfortable while still keeping the pressure on them for speedy deal closure.

You have probably heard this phrase before: All the roads lead to Rome! Sooner or later during the sales cycle, you may find yourself here at the closing phase. That is, you will see yourself at this stage shortly after an unsuccessful prospecting or qualification round or after successful rounds of presentations and negotiation.

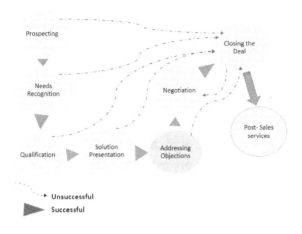

Figure 9.

Unless a magical decision maker shows up desperate to dump cash on your desk, you, like all of us, must patiently go through the phases examined in this book and depicted in the flow-chart above. Figure 9 also shows the closing phase as the most logical end point for other earlier phases. Of course, the goal from the prospecting phase on is to get to closing so your buyer signs the contract and you finalize the deal. However, *assumptive* closing or aggressive closing questions may derail the deal and run off any potential buyer. Thus, once you're confident that the solution you're providing will fully fit the buyer's needs, it's time to ask for the sale. Make sure your buyer feels comfortable with your offerings, so you won't be afraid to communicate your desire to move the deal forward.

As Michael Bosworth described in *Solution Selling*, "Each firm won because it leveraged its ability to create appealing customer value faster, better, and less expensive than did the larger and better known and better financed competitors."[1] As we said earlier, the trust, credibility, integrity, and passion the seller demonstrates in each phase of the sales process can help build a meaningful relationship with the prospect along this customer building journey. According to Qvella's CEO:

> There are two elements to this: 1) the relationship the salesperson makes with the decision maker and how much trust is built between them, especially for a high-ticket purchase, 2) how much trust the prospect has in the company. In other words, do they believe the numbers they put out and will they stand behind their product? And more importantly, what level of care and service will they provide after the sale.

Closing With Success

As per *Solution Selling*, once you empower your buyer and you gave them a sense of control, they will not feel they are being sold to. Instead, they own the value justification, with its foundation (as we described in the previous chapter) rooted in the prospect's challenges and an action vision. When your presentation(s) and demonstrations factually convince buyers of the benefits and the longevity of your solution, they will be emotionally ready to buy. As a result, most challenges have been addressed and all the sales cycle phases have been successful. Both the seller and the buyer have agreed to terms and are ready to close. The only potential challenges would be on-time delivery, implementation, and the payment plan for your solution—either in full or partial. Meanwhile, inform your sales management staff so they can prepare the needed paperwork, which would have to do with finance, legal matters, and logistics.

Closing Strategy: Hard vs. Soft

In earlier chapters, I warned you about celebrating too early; that is, don't close before it is *closed*. Do you still remember the iceberg metaphor—most of its surface is not visible? Hidden under the surface are other stakeholders' sentiments toward your offering, newly surfaced budgetary constraints, Covid-19 like pandemics, current and future legal obligations, etc., which all can play a significant role in the buyer's final decision. These and other micro- and macro-economic risks are well beyond your and your management's control. Some of these issues could have been dealt with in parallel during the earlier phases. But they were not. As a result, you are walking a fine line in picking a closing strategy. You are left trying to determine if the buyer has a legitimate reason to delay signing or is stalling to shop around for a better deal.

In a *Harvard Business Review* article, Steve W. Martin, profes-sor of sales strategy at USC, revealed, based on study results, that using "*hard close*" techniques such as "This is the last time we'll be able to extend this offer" or aggressively asserting "We need an answer now!" are the least effective ways to close a deal.[2]

Instead, let's go back to the question strategies mentioned ear-lier. A close-ended question which merely seeks a "yes" or "no" answer does not leave an alternate action to salvage a deal. It is pretty much tantamount to the proverbial "take it or leave it" ultimatum which no potential buyer would appreciate. Instead, the "*soft closing*" technique, which uses non-aggressive closing coupled with well-crafted open-ended questions, will make the buyer feel more comfortable, while still exerting pressure to move forward.

Facilitating Decisions Instead of Manipulating

The solution selling approach championed by Michael Bosworth reminds us that the buyers must direct themselves and arrive at the purchasing opportunity when they are ready. You as the seller have served them well both as a trusted advisor and as a buying facilitator during the previous phases. So, you must prepare to close the sale in a way that shows respect for the buyer's emotions and decision-making logic.

By wading through the earlier phases and reaching the closing stage, you have gained valuable situational fluency which includes situational and capability knowledge, people, and selling skills. Also, you know the purchaser's pain, challenges, and where they want to see themselves. You know how they want to serve their stakeholders and how your solution fits into that need.

It is a given that you know more than anyone about your products and competitive landscape. Knowing more than your buyers about their competitions can greatly help you enumerate and quantify the financial disadvantages if they decide to pass on the deal at hand. Thus, your confidence buoyed by your wealth of knowledge and fluency will motivate you to push forward with the *soft-closing* strategy. That is, without any manipulative intentions, you need to present your buyer with a series of questions to identify their commitment to closing the deal.

Here are some pointed soft-closing questions recommended by Geoffrey James, the co-author of *Scientific Selling*. In his *Inc.* magazine article, he said every seller should be able to master these few classic ways to close a deal.[3]

1. The Assumptive Close

Example: "Help me understand your process and how your company will purchase this product."

Best Use: When you're not certain that the customer is convinced. Talking about the details will either confirm the customer's decision to buy or allow for further discussion. Be careful with this one, though—if your delivery is too ham-handed, this close can seem manipulative.

2. The Reverse Close

Example: "Is there any reason, if we gave you the product at this price, that you wouldn't do business with our company?"

Best Use: When the customer has a pessimistic personality and enjoys nit-picking and finding fault. Remember to have a backup plan if the answer is "Yes, which is why I'm not going to buy."

3. The Time-Sensitive Close

Example: "You said you want to get this done by a certain time and date. Let's look at our calendars and figure out what we need to do today."

Best Use: When the customer has committed to achieving a specific goal within a specific time. This is also useful as an intermediate close on the next step to lay the groundwork for a final close.

4. The Direct-Question Close

Example: "It looks like we've answered all your questions. Shall we move forward with this?"

Best Use: This is a general purpose close and can be applied in almost any sales situation. It never seems manipulative and seldom backfires. Should the answer be no, then start a conversation that investigates why the customer isn't yet ready to buy.

5. The Direct-Statement Close

Example: "Let's move forward on this."

Best Use: Use this when you've received multiple green lights signaling that the customer is ready to buy. This close has an added benefit—positioning the purchase as an agreement between equals, rather than a supplication from the seller to the buyer.

Secure a Commitment:

Based on additional insights, objections, requests that the soft-closing questions elicited from the buyer, you can take the appropriate action by trying these steps recommended in *Question that Sell* by Paul Cherry:

1. **Find a point of agreement:**

    Regardless of what the customer's new objection is, always find some point of agreement you can work from. If the complaint is about the price, instead of countering the claim, try to find some element within their statement that you agree with. And then move on to the next topic.

2. **Offer a question to clarify:**

    You want to ask more focused, rather than open-ended questions that will cut into the core of the buyer's problem and lead to better outcome.

3. **Educate the customer:**

    In the earlier opportunities you provided the buyer with ample information, POC, and success stories on how your solution has helped other satisfied customers. Nevertheless, more reassurances on the features and benefits of your solution are needed to help them envision it helping them overcome their current challenges. [4]

The outcome of each of the above actions will send you back to one of the previous phases—indicating that the activities in those phases were not executed thoroughly and successfully. At the end, if you still see stalling with no movement toward closing the deal, it is important to cut your losses and walk away. Yes, it's painful, but in many cases, your time—and your teams' time—are better spent on more promising opportunities.

Before you close the book on dud deals, make sure you understand the reasons the deal did not close. Collectively with your inside champion, roll up your sleeves and look at what you missed and what you can do to improve, so the next opportunity will have a successful outcome. In the next section, we look at a study that reveals some of the reasons deals fail.

Reasons Deals Go Bad:

What were the lessons learned from your recent sales opportunity that did not close? Were you able to discern what went well and what did not? Did your management, peers, or inside champion offer any mentorship or advice? According to Steve W. Martin, professor of sales strategy at USC, there are several reasons salespeople don't close deals. In fact, we have implicitly and explicitly talked about many of them throughout the book; however, it would be a good review to list them again here.[2]

1. **The salesperson is not trusted or respected.** Customers can think of a salesperson as someone who is trying to sell something, a supplier with whom they do business, a strategic partner who is important to their business, or a trusted adviser. However, just 18 percent of salespeople buyers met over the past year would be classified as trusted advisers whom they respect.

2. **The salesperson can't communicate effectively with senior executives.** The rare conversations they have with C-suite decision makers directly determine whether they win or lose the deal. Unfortunately, buyers report that less than one out of three salespeople can hold an effective conversation with a senior executive.

3. **The salesperson can't clearly explain how their solution helps the buyer's business.** Buyers amass information that helps them justify their strategic decisions. However, buyers say only 54 percent of salespeople they meet with can clearly explain how their solution helps the buyer's business.

4. **The salesperson is too self-centered.** Survey participants revealed that they feel pressured by self-centered salespeople. Forty-four percent believed salespeople are only serving their own agenda, while 25 percent indicated salespeople only care about making the sale.

5. **The salesperson used the wrong closing strategy.** A hard close creates a binary "*yes or no*" response from the buyer; therefore, may kill the deal. Soft close techniques such as "If you spend another $100,000, you will receive an additional 10 percent off the entire order" were rated most effective. A soft close leads buyers to believe they are in control.

6. **The salesperson didn't alleviate the risks associated with buying their solution.** Business-to-business buyers are fixated on risk mitigation and are skeptical based on past interactions. But still, one of the primary reasons for walking away after a lengthy evaluation is because the salesperson hasn't mitigated

the risk of buying. Salespeople should understand these dynamics as they seek to assuage buyers' concerns about risk.

7. **The salesperson can't establish a personal connection with the buyer.** Buyers cited five key reasons why there isn't "chemistry" or a personal connection with a particular salesperson:

- The salesperson was too pushy.
- The salesperson had an incompatible communication style.
- The salesperson's personality was much different from the buyer's.
- The salesperson was too eager to befriend the buyer.
- The salesperson was too old or too young.

Most salespeople are very comfortable selling to certain types of people. However, they're far less likely to establish rapport with someone who is wired differently than themselves.

In the previous chapter, we strongly suggested that no negotiation should end with a "no." The same principle applies here too; we should never let any selling endeavor end on a "no." That is, if talks failed after the solution presentation round, we must know why. For example, if the deal broke down, was it because of focusing too much on certain features or benefits that your subject matter expert(s) or the technical staff believed were important, yet they had nothing to do with the needs of the buyer? Or the sales guide was put together by the marketing department and did not adequately position your offerings in the competitive landscape. Or was it because you were not able to defend the price and defuse pricing concerns and objections during the negotiation round? Whatever the reasons for terminating the deal, earnest efforts must be made to get answers explaining the whys and sharing the lessons learned with the marketing, technical staff, or the teams and departments involved to boost the success of future sales endeavors. As the Nobel Prize winner Louise Glück says in one of her poems, "*Where the leap forward is made from a deep sense of loss.*"

Embrace for More Deals to be Started and Closed Virtually

First and foremost, the sellers and their sales organizations must be in a position to avert business stoppage by eliminating any Single Point of Failure (SPOF) within their sales operations. For example, any political or natural calamity or even during the COVID lockdown—that we are currently in the midst of it—relying on a single modality of face-to face sales operation may ground your business. An extensive study by the San Jose [California] *Mercury News* reported that when the pandemic finally ends, entrepreneurs, engineers, and experts—which constitute many of your prospects and potential customers—agree that one thing is clear: Silicon Valley [San Jose and the San Francisco's South Bay Area of California] will never be the same.[6] Undoubtedly, some worry that the culture of collaboration and sales relationship will suffer without face-to-face encounters. However, in many respects, there is no way to go back; thus, as it was emphasized almost in each chapter, the sellers must embrace the reality of working and delivering virtually. This is one of the few ways—but the most effective one—to move away from the pack of your competitions. "Successful companies will be those that can nurture talent and build a strong culture while taking advantage of opportunities remote work presents," according to Peter Rojas, California Bay Area venture capitalist at Betaworks. His firm invested in more than 100 companies—and none appear hurt by the shift to remote; and as he claimed: "everybody adjusted and figured out how to get their stuff done [remotely]."

Also, Kaye Gitibin, the CEO of Go Rental—an elite car rental service around the US—saw his business suffered in the early months of pandemic; however, they had to get back on their feet, trying many of their sales and marketing tasks—in a purely face-to-face business landscape—remotely. According to him, "Since the pandemic, we had to make some adjustments in interacting with our prospects. Our success was based on making eye contact, smiling, and shaking hands, but we could not do that on video. We had to overcome these challenges to stay ahead of the competition. How do we build relationships via phone and email and get them ready for our video conferencing? How do we break the ice? How do we keep them engaged during the virtual meeting? These are the areas that we had no experience in. But, we have noticed that since the majority of the executives are working from home or are isolated in their offices, they have more time to interact. We have been able to create more partnership during the virtual meeting era, pandemic, than before. Keeping the level of engagement with our prospect, creating a meaningful relationship prior to our video conferencing, following up, and following through after the virtual meeting has been our success during this era."

So, at the risk of any misconstruing by the readers that this book is the promoter of remote selling by going through the phases virtually, it is very important that the sellers and their organizations must realize that the days of some of the face-to-face sales activities are numbered.

In fact, many corporate heavyweights today are adamant about working and selling remote from home. A year after the COVID pandemic started, Marc Benioff, the chairman and CEO of Salesforce.com, a cloud-based software company which provides CRM services to many small and big companies, in an interview with a financial TV network (CNBS, January 2021) revealed that his company had revised their last year's business plan and wrote an entirely different one based on three main ideas. Regarding one of those ideas, he stated that, "we all have been working and living at home, so we need to be selling and marketing from home, servicing and e-commencing from home and we need to collaborate from home". These expectations were the main impetus for his company to go and buy a channel-based messaging company for $27 billion for better remote collaborations.

Of course, there are many recent examples of how the legacy industry establishments failed to adapt and embrace the new ways of doing business. On top of the list, we have the saga of Blockbuster video rental with 2,800 brick-and-mortar locations and $8.4 billion valuation in 1994- just to fade away and allow a much smaller rival but virtual and cloud-based company called Netflix to lead the video-on-demand market with $203 billion cap in 2020.

The quote below attests to the above reality that: "It is not the strongest of the species that survives, nor the most intelligent that survives. It is the one that is most adaptable to change." Many believe this is a quote from Charles Darwin on the theory of evolution; others disagree. But regardless of who offered this wisdom, its core message should compel us to embrace and respect the digital transformation that is taking place in commerce today.

After the Close!

As part of the deal closing, instead of doing a victory lap, we need to measure how the solution really helped the customer. Extracting the ROI will help us sell more in the future. How your next client looks based on these ROIs is an advertisement for you.[5] This will lead to more ammunition for talking to other potential buyers. That is, you can talk about the case studies, success stories, and tangible data, which will improve future sales and marketing efforts. Again, the key point is when the marketing and sales forces working together, they can achieve much more than a salesperson working solo.

Post-Sales Support

Morris A. Cohen, *et. al*, tell us in their *Harvard Business Review* article that, "This is the golden age of services, and to survive and prosper, we're told, every company must transform itself into a service business."[7] To illustrate this, have you bought something the sellers did not promise superior post-sales service and support for—better than their competition? Of course, all vendors and suppliers tout their post-sale incentives. Thus, the last word here in the final stage of the sales process will be about post-sales activities, to be specific, the support and services promised to the customer during the earlier phases by the seller.

Of course, touting and bragging about your exceptional post-sales support and services may not be enough for the savvy customers. For years, the sales leaders- across all industries- have been focusing on offering a *differentiated* or a *premium* type of service to their customers. As a Senior VP of sales & Marketing at Infineon Technologies, Shawn Slusser was one of the main advocates and evangelist of these such programs based on his company's main credos of *"winning customers' hearts"*. Remember, in the Prospecting and Discovery chapters we pointed to the psychology of buying where customers use emotions for any purchase decisions which will be backed by logical calculations and assessments in their brains. As part of promoting these types of services, Slusser first defines the terms *Services* vs. *Service* before dive into the core of the premium service. Aside from the fact that one is the plural form of the other, for many sellers and buyers, their meanings may be intuitive or perhaps trivial; however, his definitions remind businesses the true essence of these two overused words in the world of sales today:

> *"Services* are the specific support activities we offer: Tech support, logistics, quality support which of course, very valuable to our customers. On the other hand, *Service* is how we make the customer feel: understood and appreciated. Both are the main pillars of the *premium service* culture; and once we have them working together at the highest levels it becomes a huge advantage in helping us to win business with the returned customers who are willing to pay a little bit more."

All in all, the Infineon corporate executives in Munich and Americas strongly believe that the visceral practice of such service will eventually lead the sales teams to: 1) realizing higher profitability, 2) gaining acknowledgement for the extra effort, and 3) increasing customer loyalty.

Executives swear by the services-centric view of the world, but privately, they admit to one niggling concern: Most companies either don't know how to or don't care to provide after-sales service effectively. But remember, as businesses began offering solutions instead of products, it became evident that selling spare parts and after-sales repairs, installing upgrades, reconditioning equipment, carrying out inspections, day-to-day maintenance, offering technical support, consulting, training, and arranging finances could be a bountiful source of revenue and profits as well. In fact, "After-sales services are a high-margin business, and they account for a large chunk of corporate profits."[7]

For example, Boeing is the world's largest aerospace and defense ompany. With headquarters in Chicago, the firm operates in four segments, commercial airplanes, global services, defense, space, and security, and Boeing capital. Boeing's commercial airplane segment produces about 60 percent of their sales and two-thirds of their operating profit. Also, its global services segment provides aftermarket service to commercial and military aircraft and produces about 15 percent of sales and 21 percent of operating profit,[8] which can't be ignored by any sales or marketing organization.

An Accenture study revealed that General Motors (GM) earned more profits from $9 billion in after-sales revenues in

2001 than it did from $150 billion of income from car sales. Wall Street tracks companies' aftermarket prowess, and studies show that there's a direct correlation between stock prices and the quality of a firms' after-sales service. So, it is no wonder that many experts believe good product support is smart marketing.

Aside from these legacy-heavy industry giants, many digital companies, such as Amazon, have been fostering their customer success (or customer experience) by providing post-sale support. The SE senior manager at Oracle tells us, "This is beyond good customer service, especially if the nature of sales is technical; focusing on customer success requires a very technical team to be in synch with customers from 'pitch to production' as we call it." By actually including professional services and project management with most deals, the opportunities to upsell and cross-sell increase. Else, "If we don't do it, stuff never gets implemented correctly, and customers give up or, at best, never renew the contract," as the sales director pointed out.

Tackling Aftermarket Challenges

As stated above, for Boeing and GM, after-sales services are a high-margin business, and they account for a large chunk of corporate profits; nevertheless, companies find it tough to compete in the aftermarket. Across industries, delivering after-sales services is more complex than manufacturing products. On top of that, companies have to handle—in an environmentally safe fashion—the return, repair, and disposal of failed components.

Most businesses don't appreciate the myriad challenges. A research shows that to win in the aftermarket, executives need to recognize that after-sales service is a commitment companies make to respond within a specific time to the customer's need for support:

1. Companies must approach the promises they make as products they design, price, produce, and deliver to customers to generate revenue.
2. Companies must design a portfolio of service products.
3. Companies should visualize a distinctive after-sales service supply chain that delivers services to customers through a network of resources.[7]

Summary

The deal closing phase is the logical endpoint for all earlier phases.

- Regardless of how successful or unsuccessful sellers were in the early phases, they will end up here in this phase.
- It is understandable for sellers to be afraid to ask for a sale because they are worried about hearing "no"—resulting all their hard work developing the opportunity being wasted.
- Regardless of how confident you are, never ask for the sale until you cannot think of a single reason the buyer can't or will not buy today.
- In many cases, buyer have legitimate reasons to delay closing, which are beyond your and your management's control.
- If the buyer stalls, soft-closing strategies are preferred over hard-closing tactics.

- Salespeople use soft-closing questions which require direct answers to seal the deal.
- To secure commitment and unearth buyer's motivation from their responses, sellers should:
  - » Find a point of agreement.
  - » Offer a question to clarify.
  - » Educate the customer.
- Research tells us there are seven key reasons salespeople can't close a deal.
- Even after the coronavirus pandemic ends, many CEOs are expecting their workforce to work remotely; thus, more and more deals must be closed virtually.
- After-sales services are high-margin, and they account for a large chunk of corporate profits.
- There's a distinct correlation between the quality of after-sales service and customer intent to repurchase.
- If done right, post-sales service and support will bring much need profit to the sales organization.

Call2Action

- Ask your peers or sales management team for documents, notes, and/or lessons learned from failed deals.
- Share the seven reasons from Steve W. Martin research with your peers to see if they concur.
- Seek coaching on one or more of the areas the seven reasons alluded to.

Bibliography

[1]: *Solution Selling*. Michael T. Bosworth. McGraw-Hill Publishing.

[2]: "7 Reasons Salespeople Don't Close the Deal." Steve W. Martin. *Harvard Business Review.* August 2017.

[3]: "5 Ways to Close a Deal." Geoffrey James. *Inc. Magazine,* September 2012.

[4]: *Question That Sell.* Paul Cherry.

[5]: "Is the Best Sales Tool an ROI Calculator?" John Cerqueira, Episode 65, Aslan Sales Training Group.

[6]: "Does Remote Work Hurt Valley's Tech Innovation?" Than Baron. *San Jose Mercury News.* December 13, 2020.

[7]: "Winning in the Aftermarket." Morris A. Cohen, Narendra Agrawal, and Vipul Agrawal. *Harvard Business Review.* May 2006.

[8]: "Analyst Report: The Boeing Company." Burkett Huey, Morningstar Equity Analyst Report. September 2020.

Acknowledgments

Although my journey to the world of sales and marketing started with my first sales job right after college, every cold call and customer interaction was a chore- merely a shot in a dark. During my product marketing and technical training years, everything made sense on paper and on slides. But it was not until entering an executive MBA program that I was able to connect the dots and truly fathom the business, financial, and strategical reasons behind organizational and corporate decisions taken during my career in more than half-dozen companies that I worked for. So, great thanks to the faculty and staff of School of Economics and Business Administration of Saints Mary's College of California. A big part of that program was our Saturday breakfast club with my ten cohorts. Thank you all for your motivation, inspiration, and feedback during our eighteen months of studying together.

Also, thanks to the head of Infineon's Sales and Marketing Academy (SaMA) in Munich, Germany, for taking a risk on me and giving a purely technical person a sales enablement role. I would not have been able to survive in this role without the continued support and guidance from our global SaMA, SMT, and SMD team members. Thank you, folks, in Singapore, Beijing, Tokyo, Porto, Munich, Milpitas, and El Segundo!

Finally, to write this book, I sat on the shoulders of few sales and marketing executives—some giants in their field. Shaun Karamdashti, the Cloud Solutions and Engineering Sales Senior Manager at Oracle, with his valuable customer experience provided great contributions to the prospecting and qualification chapters. As a great soccer center back, I always had his back at the goal line, so this was the most opportune time for him to return the favor with his great suggestions and steering the topics of new areas of sales challenges. My dear friend, Hamid Karimi, the VP of technology alliances with OPSWAT has always been a source of inspiration and motivation for me going back to the days of working together at SCO Unix. His insight and suggestions really shaped the sales enablement section of this book, and I'm hoping that we can collaborate on this specific topic in the near future.

Many thanks and much appreciation to my dear friend Dr. Alavi in Toronto, Canada, who played a great role in shaping the topics in the prospecting, objection and negotiation. Tino, since the days of our graduate studies and working together in the same electro-photonic lab at Florida Tech, has always been a true serial entrepreneur—well before this buzz word became part of today's hi-tech nomenclature. His superb experimental abilities and business acumen made him a successful scientist and CEO of Qvella Corp. Also, from within the same medical device company, great stories and words of wisdom were contributed by the VP of Sales, Glen Magnus, which made many of the concepts clearer.

The first time I brought up the topic of this book was during the FIFA World Cup trip to Russia. Mehdy Khotan embraced the idea and became a big supporter and major contributor to this book. As a veteran marketing executive within the semiconductor industry, previously with Maxim, his many stories on various sales challenges and best practices are greatly appreciated. Also, I am very grateful to Hamed Emami, the sales director of Cadence Design Systems. The valuable sales content and resources he provided along with awareness of certain sales challenges through role-playing were priceless.

Brett Clay, the author of two bestselling sales books, *Forceful Selling* and *Selling Changes and a Management Consultant* was a great motivator. Brett's guidance, mentorship, and pearls of wisdom continuously helped me to better identify my audience—something only an executive coach and business school lecturer can bring to the table. Also, Brett was the nexus to find my expert editor, Dr. Tyler Tichelaar of Superior Book Productions. As an accomplished author and publisher, he expressed my thoughts and words much more eloquently and intuitively than I ever could. For that, I'm always grateful to him. I also would like to thank my author coach Ms. Anne Jazner of Cuesta Park Consulting for great tips on graphics and more effective communication with my readers.

Hamid Nouri the managing principal and executive director of AgiLeanIT contributed greatly to the discovery and need analysis chapter, and in particular, the section on RFP. Thank you, Hamid, for making this chapter richer with all your lessons learned across a wide variety of industries from healthcare to financial services.

Diana Davis, Ivonne Duenas, Ani Boghossian Fayezi, Tamara Heat-Underbrink, Allie Fayezi, Bob Darafshi, Christopher Davis, Julius Sarkis, Diane Pinto, Kaye Gitibin, Dr Joel Block, Heiko Schickel, Christop von Schierstaedt, Nazanin Imani, Dr. Mani Mina, Neil Cashell, Lori Alvin, Farshid Oshidari, Haleh Aminfayezi, Borz Pourabbas, Neekaan Oshidary, Dr. Sid Mohaseb, Shadi Razifard, Mohsen Hossieni, Dr. Andre Peine, Patrick Reardon, H.F. Ghazvini, Shawn Slusser, Till Hans, Sandra Kirchharz, Ivan Banderas, Tim Van Sciver, Samieh Behnam, Dominik Schott, and Dr. Saeed Attar, I can't thank you enough folks for the tremendous support each of you provided me during the writing of this book by sharing years of your industry and academic expertise and experiences. Also, thanks to my publisher Outskirt Press. Monica Harman, my publishing consultant, and my author representatives Deni Sinteral-Scott. While educating me along the way on many complex aspects of publication choices and decisions, Deni moved this endeavor to the finish line patiently and expertly. Also, my sincere thanks to my graphic artists, Yasi Rezai, Kaveh and Farzin Nikpour whose images and drawings gave more meanings and context to the various topics in different chapters.

I am, and will always be, indebted to Dr. Hamid Elahi, former general manager of Energy Consulting Group at General Electric (GE) for various important roles that he has played in my life. From proof-reading my very first English papers in high school to this manuscript, nothing has changed! His attention to details and looking out for ease of comprehension by the reader have always made me go through the Nth drafts and edits. His industry and consulting views were instrumental shaping the introduction of this book.

Last but not least, to get to where I am now- as a trainer, teacher and a coach- I owe it all to the things that I have learned from each and every student, colleague, and customer whom I've crossed paths. I salute you!

About the Author

Ramin Elahi has been an educator, trainer, and coach for most of his career, which spans twenty-plus years. His early years as a support, escalation, and application engineer prepared him technically so his networking, data center, and cloud storage architecture classes and seminars are filled with leading edge technology concepts and trends. He has been passionate about learning and development using any delivery modalities from ILT (Instructor Led Training) to virtual. He augments course technical content with customer service experience, real-life lessons learned, and industry best practices. He

holds undergraduate and graduate degrees in electrical engineering from Iowa State University and Florida Institute of Technology, respectively, and earned his executive MBA from St. Mary's

College of California. He is currently the sales training portfolio manager at Infineon Technologies and an adjunct faculty instructor at the University of California Santa Cruz extension. He lives with his wife and two daughters in San Jose, California.

CPSIA information can be obtained
at www.ICGtesting.com
Printed in the USA
BVHW091405260421
605865BV00011B/2244